Edited by Alan Durband

SECOND
PLAYBILL THREE

Hutchinson Educational

HUTCHINSON EDUCATIONAL LTD
3 Fitzroy Square, London W1

London Melbourne Sydney Auckland
Wellington Johannesburg Cape Town
and agencies throughout the world

First published 1973

*This book has been set in Bembo type, printed in Great Britain
on smooth wove paper by Anchor Press, and
bound by Wm. Brendon, both of Tiptree, Essex*

ISBN 0 09 113500 1 (C)
113501 X (P)

...COLLE...

Second Playbill ...hree

...Y

The *Playbill* series brings to...ew, specially
commissioned or adapted plays for use in schools.
The emphasis is ...rn book on or before latest date ...the
theatre and alli... stamped below ...ed media. The volumes are graded
in difficulty.

Books by Alan Durband

ENGLISH WORKSHOP 1–3
CONTEMPORARY ENGLISH 1–2
SHORTER CONTEMPORARY ENGLISH
NEW ENGLISH 1–4

Edited by Alan Durband

NEW DIRECTIONS
Five one-act plays in the modern idiom
PLAYBILL 1–3
SECOND PLAYBILL 1–3

Contents

Introduction

Second Playbill Three contains plays by Don Shaw, Charles Wood, Charles Dyer, David Selbourne and Henry Livings.

1 *The Plays*

Don Shaw's *Me Mackenna* is an adaptation for the stage of the original TV play. Mackenna is a vicious, foul-mouthed barrack-room bully: there is no place in his mean understanding for a young man like Moore who wants to leave the Army for the Church. Smouldering inside Mackenna is a burning resentment against authority and a bitter sense of injustice because he has been punished for assaulting an officer. He sets out to expose Moore as a sham, and his method is crude and sadistic. Aided by Davo and Bucker, whom he dominates, he ties Moore to a hot stove: 'Ter be a priest you should have ter prove you're ready to die on the Cross. Or stand the flames of Hell'. To be released, Moore has to deny the existence of God. As he is tormented with the heat, Mackenna, Davo and Bucker play cards beneath his tortured body like the soldiers beneath the Cross. Consumed with hatred, Mackenna has no pity; but Davo has, and Moore is spared from further physical suffering. In spite of his burns, Moore bears no resentment. Second Lieutenant Auden, therefore, cannot find the evidence that will bring Mackenna the punishment he deserves. Mackenna's inner torment, all the greater now, seeks relief in an ultimate confrontation. He mounts the hot stove himself to prove that 'nobody beats Mackenna'—not the faith of a weakling priest, nor

even the flames of Hell. But Moore's compassion is total.
What he will not do to save himself, he will do for the
brutal Mackenna. Mackenna, invincibly ignorant, boasts of
victory.

Charles Wood's *Tie Up the Ballcock* is also based on violence.
An atom bomb is supposed to have fallen, and a Civil Defence
exercise is in full swing. Casualties lie amongst the ruins. A
soup kitchen stands at the ready. Worthy citizens like Mr
Carver and Chats Harris busy themselves in the rubble.
Their farcical activities are contrasted with the increasingly
menacing reality of nuclear war. Bessie and Alexandra, the
kitchen ladies, perform a music-hall sequence based on a sick
joke while the boy and girl, potentially a romantic couple,
encounter the horrors of radiation burns and a real casualty.
The exercise begins as an adult war-game with worthy
intentions. It ends as a nightmare glimpse of atomic disaster,
far removed from the inanely helpful hint on plumbing which
gives the play its satirical title.

Charles Dyer's *A Hot Godly Wind* is a modern morality
play set around a hole. Harry has dug hundreds of holes in
his lifetime and never known the reason why. He struggles
for perfection in his work, but despite a superficial jocularity
and a zest for words, he has 'niggling doubts' because of a
recurrent element of failure. Harry's mate George is living
evidence of the shortness of mortal life—'our allotted span
is but a finger-click against eternity'—but as a senior citizen
he is in a particularly hopeless situation: what can the old
folk do to improve the lot of the little people who, over the
generations, have suffered so much? Eric, the trumpeter of
Truth, has a mission to 'show people the way and make them
happy'. He is on strike for better conditions, and protests that

'everything is dark from the shade of cancerous offices'. Instead of building homes, men are concerned only to make money, forgetful of the consequences of overpopulation, the by-product of the sex drive personified by Tom. Tom, lustful and virile, is an inveterate womaniser—but he is also the spirit of Everyman when, serious for a moment, he wonders whether he and his companions stand on the edge of the hole as if in balance between Heaven and Hell. The Postman disagrees with everyone. He rejects the 'holy pink' of Eric's truth and finds it too depressing. He stands for Argument, and helps to nudge the minds of people like Harry who are trying to discover themselves. As the Postman says, 'miracles don't shine from Holes'; but at least Harry the Mediocre can face reality and aspire to a better future. Perhaps, after all, a 'hot godly wind' has blown.

The relationships explored in David Selbourne's *Class Play* are much more terrestrial. John, Fred and Kate are three fifteen-year-olds united only in that they all hate school. Their future is unattractive and they fear it; they are bored; they lack hope and have no ambition. They fluctuate emotionally between liking each other and hating each other. In ten short scenes they inter-act, speaking their private thoughts aloud, exploring their teenage feelings, and forming patterns as they move together or part, according to their relationships. Happiness eludes them. The lovely future to which Kate aspires is rejected by John because to him it means kids, dishcloths, cooking and bingo; but Fred, albeit in isolation, has some faith. 'We've got a future,' he says. 'We all have.' But they stand apart.

Henry Livings' *Brainscrew* is another dramatic exercise in personal exploration. Harry Steadman is a TV personality—

an extrovert with a plastic smile and a ready quip. He takes part in a panel game chaired by the smooth, professional Alisdair Mendip. Mary Hass, his fellow contestant, plays the game of *Brainscrew* to win it, come what may. The idea of the game is that one contestant dreams up a set of circumstances, and the other has to find out what the circumstances are. After a normal first round in which Harry has placed himself in a belfry, it is Mary's turn. She is business-like from the start, and gradually Harry's self-confidence, so publicly successful in the first round, is eroded as he finds himself in circumstances loaded with menace, horror and insecurity. Slowly the side of his character he has so skilfully concealed is exposed; he finds himself moving inexorably towards a reality which represents the real Harry Steadman. It comes as a shock to him to find that the circumstances in this round of the game are actually of his own making, not Mary's. What the audience has been watching is 'Harry Steadman, here and now': for once in his brash life a total victim of the medium which normally sustains him.

2 *The Playwrights*

Don Shaw was born in 1934. He went to the military academy at Sandhurst, where he lived with the Duke of Kent, King Hussein of Jordan, and King Feisal of Iraq. In spite of this, he says he still finds class attitudes unbearable, and describes himself as 'a liberal with a puritanical streak; a socialist voter with a conservative instinct'. He has acted at Derby Playhouse, on BBC radio, and he was a founder member of Derby Theatre-in-the-Round. He has been a loyal supporter of Derby County since he was ten years old, and his only relaxation is watching the club on winter Saturday afternoons. All his spare time is devoted to writing—he has written thirty

TV plays in the last three years. For twelve years he taught the deaf and partially-hearing. At present he is teaching in a grammar school. His ambition is to keep writing.

Charles Wood is another playwright with military connections. Born in 1932, he spent five years as a regular soldier between 1950 and 1955. His parents were on the stage, and he has himself been both a scenic designer and a stage manager in the professional theatre. His first TV play to be produced (in 1961) was *Traitor in a Steel Helmet*, followed by *Prisoner and Escort*, which was also adapted for the stage. His principal plays include *Fill the Stage with Happy Hours* and *Dingo* (written for the National Theatre). He is equally well known for his film-scripts: *How I Won the War*, *The Charge of the Light Brigade*, and for the Beatles' *Help!*

Charles Dyer's plays are performed throughout the world, and his novels are published in many languages. He is noted for the humanity and depth of his characters, and for his plays upon the theme of loneliness. *Rattle of a Simple Man* is a classic of contemporary theatre; *Staircase*, written for the Royal Shakespeare Company and later filmed, firmly established him as a master of the duologue. He is married to actress Fiona Thomson, and they live in Buckinghamshire with their three young sons John, Peter and Timothy, to whom *A Hot Godly Wind* is dedicated.

David Selbourne was born in London in 1937, but his upbringing was in Lancashire. His first full-length play to be professionally staged was *The Play of William Cooper and Edmund Dew-Nevett* at the Northcott Theatre, Exeter, in 1968. The Liverpool Everyman presented his *Two-Backed Beast* in 1969, and *Dorabella* was presented at the Edinburgh Festival in the following year. He is now a tutor at Ruskin College, Oxford.

Henry Livings was born in 1929 at Prestwich, Lancashire. He enjoys time spent in towns, and lives in the Yorkshire industrial village of Dobcross. He served in the RAF, attended Liverpool University, worked in a hosiery factory and a hotel, and spent some years as a professional actor with Joan Littlewood and Theatre Workshop. He still acts locally in rep, on radio and on TV; his association with Alex Glasgow and *Northern Drift* has led to many BBC2 appearances. His first play, *Jack's Horrible Luck*, was sold to the BBC in 1959. In 1961 he won the Evening Standard Drama Award with *Stop It, Whoever You Are*, and in 1965 he won the Britannica Award with *Kelley's Eye*. His other plays include *Big Soft Nellie, Nil Carborundum, Eh?* (filmed by Peter Hall as *Work is a Four-Letter Word*) and *The Little Mrs Foster Show*. He has also many TV and radio plays to his credit.

Acknowledgements

For permission to publish the plays in this volume, the editor is grateful to the following authors and their agents: Don Shaw and Peter Crouch Plays Ltd for *Me Mackenna*; Charles Wood and Margaret Ramsay Ltd for *Tie Up the Ballcock*; Charles Dyer and Eric Glass Ltd for *A Hot Godly Wind*; David Selbourne and John Calder Ltd for *Class Play*; Henry Livings and Margaret Ramsay Ltd for *Brainscrew*.

No performance of these plays may be given unless a licence has been obtained. Applications should be addressed to the authors' agents.

Me Mackenna

DON SHAW

CAST

BUCKER
DAVO
MOORE
MACKENNA
SECOND LIEUTENANT AUDEN

Me Mackenna

SCENE 1: *A barrack room in an Army camp. Iron beds stretch along the walls. In the centre of the room is an iron stove; the chimney leads through the apex of the roof. A dull red glow indicates that the fire is lit.*
DAVO and BUCKER are playing a leisurely game of pontoon. DAVO is a shambling, easy-going lad, completely without malice. BUCKER is a big-boned, unintelligent youth with cropped hair. Both are in denims, green pullovers, and dirty canvas shoes.
The lighting is inadequate: a single bare bulb hangs above the wooden table at which they are seated. A radio plays softly in the background.

BUCKER: Twist.

[DAVO *hands him a card*]

Aw. Bust!

[DAVO *collects his halfpenny and stacks the cards for a fresh deal. As he does so,* MOORE *enters.* DAVO *deals to* BUCKER, *who shoves his last halfpenny forward as a bet*]

Stick!

[DAVO *turns up his own cards and grins as he takes the halfpenny*]

You rotten bastard! I never had the bank once!

[BUCKER *rises, and sees* MOORE *standing at the door with his kitbag.* MOORE *is hesitant, aged about eighteen, with delicate features*] [*to* MOORE]: What's up? Want a bed?

MOORE: Yes . . . this is Holding Platoon?

DAVO: Yeh, bed over there . . . corner . . .

MOORE: Thanks . . .

[MOORE *humps his kitbag to the corner bed.* DAVO *puts the cards away in a battered holder, gets up and goes to his bed near* BUCKER. *He puts the cards away in his locker and the accumulated halfpennies in his jacket pocket*]

BUCKER: Naafi's open in ten minutes . . . lend us a tanner, Davo . . .

[DAVO *hesitates and tosses him sixpence*]

Ta. I'll see you.

[*He moves from his bed and goes out of the room.* MOORE *is unpacking and stowing his kit in his locker. Suddenly* BUCKER *re-enters with urgency*]

BUCKER: Mackenna's back!

[BUCKER *quickly hides his sixpence under one of the blankets on an empty bed and quickly lies down, simulating relaxation.*

MACKENNA *enters. He is a Glaswegian; dark, squat and powerful. His short dark hair is plastered forward to a high point on his forehead. His whole being suggests menace. He wears a powder-blue drape jacket and dark trousers. His shoes are pale blue with very thick 'creeper' soles. He squelches when he moves*]

DAVO [*lightly, but with strain*]: Hello, Mack? Thought you wasn't back 'til Sunday!

MACKENNA: Where's everybody?

BUCKER: Gotta forty-eight-hour pass, Mack. 'Bout time we got one, washin' up in that lousy officers' mess.

[MACKENNA *throws himself on his bed*]

Had a good leave?

MACKENNA: Am skint an' fagged out.

BUCKER: We thought you wasn't back 'til Sunday night.

MACKENNA: That's what am tellin' youse . . . am skint. Them London bastards take all youse dough. Had ter hitch back all the way. Gotta snout, Davo?

[DAVO *fumbles and tosses* MACKENNA *a cigarette*]

Ta. Bucker? Get me a mug o' tea, eh? Had nothin' ter drink all day.

BUCKER: I ain't got no money, Mack.

MACKENNA: Lend him a tanner, Davo.

DAVO: I've just give him one.

MACKENNA: Come on you louse. Move!

[BUCKER *grimaces and reluctantly fishes out his sixpence and goes out.*

DAVO *picks up a comic and studies it carefully*]

Who's that?

[DAVO *looks up and finds* MACKENNA *looking at* MOORE]

DAVO: Dunno. Just come in.

[*He looks back at his comic*]

MACKENNA: Eh . . . eh you . . . you, soldier! Gotta light? You in the blasted corner!

[MOORE *turns to look at* MACKENNA]

Aye, you. Where you from?

MOORE: B Company. I'm sorry—I don't smoke.

MACKENNA: Say *sir* when yer talkin' ter a bleedin' officer . . .

[MOORE *does not reply.* MACKENNA *turns his head and peers at* MOORE]

Are yer deaf?

[MOORE *looks at* DAVO]

DAVO [*low*]: Say it . . .

MACKENNA: You heard what he said . . . say 'sir'. Remember where you are.

MOORE [*quiet*]: Sir.

[MACKENNA, *content, lies back. Lights his own cigarette*]

MACKENNA: Am fagged. Hitched all bloody day. An' I don't like bastards who don't smoke.

[DAVO *turns up the radio slightly, and joins in the chorus of a pop song*]

DAVO: I re-member . . . all the whi-le . . . You belong to . . .

MACKENNA: A' right, stuff it.

[DAVO *falls silent, turns the radio down again, and leaves the room.*

MOORE *takes a crucifix from the depths of his kitbag. He hesitates a moment, and then places it on his locker. He hesitates again, then kneels before the crucifix in an attitude of prayer. There is a slight pause before* MACKENNA *notices what* MOORE *is doing*]

[*Quiet*]: Eh . . .

[MACKENNA *eases himself up on one elbow*]

Eh you . . .

[MOORE *remains still*]

You know, am right, you must be deaf. What youse doin' there? Aw, fer—

MOORE [*quiet*]: I'm praying.

MACKENNA: Eh? Youse what?

[MACKENNA *rolls off his bed and pads over to stand behind* MOORE. *He sees the cross.* MOORE *is very tense*]

Well damn me. [*Viciously low*] What the hell do you think you're on?

[BUCKER *enters bearing a large mug of tea*]

BUCKER: I had to wait for the Naafi. Sorry Mack.

[BUCKER *breaks off as he sees the situation. He thinks quickly and puts the mug on the table*]

I'll be in the Naafi, Mack—

MACKENNA [*not looking*]: You stay there . . .

[BUCKER *stops*]

Looks like we've got ourselves a priest, Bucker. You know we had a flamin' priest?

BUCKER: No . . . he only just . . .

MACKENNA: Nobody told me this was a church. Allus thought this was a flamin' barrack room . . . eh Bucker?

BUCKER: Yeh.

[MACKENNA *bends and picks up the cross and moves it into the light to examine it*]

MACKENNA: What would youse say this was, eh?

BUCKER: A cross, in' it?

MACKENNA: Aye. That's wha' I thought. [*To* MOORE] Stand up. I'll count three. If you're not up I'll smash this over yer bleedin' head.

[MOORE *stands up slowly*]

MACKENNA: So what would you say, soldier . . . you know?

MOORE: It's a cross.

MACKENNA: It's a flamin' crucifix. You know who you're talking to?

MOORE: No.

MACKENNA: Let's have a look.

[*He twists* MOORE's *ears to look behind each*]

Wet as the flamin' sea. No more than four months' service. Am I right?

MOORE: Yes.

MACKENNA: Where you from?

MOORE: B Company.

MACKENNA: B Company to Holding Platoon. An' what's your move in aid of? What skive are you on? Now come on sonny, we're all in transit. That's what Holding Platoon's for, you know? Davo's being transferred to the Caterin' Corps, so he can poison the officers. Tha' right Davo? Oh

Davo's not here. What you in Holding Platoon for, Bucker, you git?

BUCKER: I dunno, Mack.

MACKENNA: Aye. An' I'm here 'cos they can think of damn all else to do wi' me, you know? So what's you. You priest, you.

MOORE: Please . . . could I have the cross back?

MACKENNA: Who the . . . he talks like . . . Eh sonny, you know when yer address an officer . . . an' when you put in a request you do it through Company Office. Answer ma question, what yer in fer? He is . . . he is deaf! He is yer know! [*Viciously low*] Tell him who he's talking to, Bucker.

BUCKER: Mackenna. Better do what he says, kidda.

[*A split second and* MACKENNA, *like lightning, seizes* MOORE *by the collar, draws his head back, and butts his forehead at* MOORE'S *nose, twice in rapid succession. But each blow stops short as* MACKENNA *makes an accompanying hard grunt, like a boxer.*

MOORE *is shaken and staggers back against the wall.* MACKENNA *grins*]

MACKENNA: An' a' didna even touch him.

[DAVO *is heard approaching singing 'Sugar Bush'*]

DAVO: 'Sugar bush I love you so . . . da dad-d-da-da . . .
    Sugar bush come dance with me . . .
    Sugar bush I love you so . . .
    I will never let you go . . . '

[DAVO *enters. He immediately senses the danger and checks*

himself. DAVO *approaches slowly. He proffers a packet of Woodbines to* MACKENNA]

DAVO: Snouts, Mack.

[MACKENNA *puts out his hand, still looking at* MOORE]

MACKENNA: Ta.

[*He takes out a cigarette slowly and puts it in his mouth*]

Light.

[BUCKER *quickly offers him a light*]

You know we gotta priest here, Davo.

DAVO: No.

MACKENNA: They sent us a priest. Wonder wha' for? He's right for it. He doesna smoke. D'yer drink? Wha's yer name?

MOORE: Moore. No, I don't.

MACKENNA: No even a sup, a wee dram you know?

MOORE: No.

MACKENNA: Women, you know? Touch of the other, eh?

MOORE: No.

MACKENNA: Tha's right then, he's a priest. Prayin' ter God all the time. Holding Platoon chaplain. Aw yeh, we don't know yet why Company Office should send us a priest, eh? You know, am sure he's dead, you know? He never seems ter hear. D'ya think he's a foreign wog, yer know?

[DAVO *shakes his head with a neutral smile*]

Bucker, ask him why's he's here. Don't move you know. Not an eye, not a finger.

[MACKENNA *retires to the table and picks up his mug of tea. He drinks and watches the group in the corner*]

DAVO: Tell him . . . he'll . . .

BUCKER: Come on, dunna muck about with him. He'll kill yer.

[MACKENNA *strolls back with his tea*]

MACKENNA: A' think this tea's pigging horrible. I'll tell you wha' I'll do—I'll pour it all down your neck if we don't find out what youse spying here fer. I'll count three . . .

MOORE: I'm being discharged.

MACKENNA: Aw now—well why the hell didn't you say! All this trouble. That's a' right then. Gotta discharge. Wha' for?

MOORE: It's not definite yet.

MACKENNA: Aw well, that's the army fer yer. Never trust . . . till it's, you know, signed.

[*He drinks his tea and studies at the same time*]

So . . . what's the discharge . . . compassionate? The old lady snuffed it?

MOORE: No.

MACKENNA: He is you know . . . he's deaf. It's like noddin' yer nut against concrete wi' this boy. Twenty bleedin' questions eh!

[*He chuckles for the first time. It's a guttural sound without any warmth whatsoever*]

Well come on! It's either the old lady's snuffed it, or youse got flat feet or dead toenails. What's yours?

MOORE: I've . . . got a religious vocation.

MACKENNA: Come again?

MOORE: I'm . . . going to be a minister in the Church of God.

MACKENNA: Get away.

MOORE: You can ask Mr Morrison.

MACKENNA: Now why should I ask him when I am asking you? Youse answering ma questions. No reason ter think you'd be lyin', yer know? Eh?

MOORE: I'm not.

MACKENNA: A' right! Stop lookin' so scared then! Nothin' ter worry youse. Course, yours is twice, you know . . . difficult.

MOORE: Sorry?

MACKENNA: I said it's twice difficult. You got first ta prove the Church of—wha? What was it?

MOORE: Church of God.

MACKENNA: Aye. You see I've never heard of any Church of God.

[MACKENNA *looks thoughtfully at* MOORE]

Aye. Well, as I see it, that's yer problem. Any twit can say am goin' ta be a priest of the Church of God, you know? An' buy a . . . crucifix . . . an' sit down, you know, and pray all flaming night. Church of God? Weird one, that! Where's that then?

MOORE: It's in Levington Street.

MACKENNA: Here? In town?

MOORE: Yes.

MACKENNA: Levington Street? I've never . . . Have you heard of Levington Street, Bucker?

BUCKER: No.

MACKENNA: Davo? You?

DAVO: Yes.

[*He sees* MACKENNA'*s look*]

No . . . no . . . I thought I had.

MACKENNA: Tha's funny, that. An' Davo, you know's, as clever a bastard you'd find this side o' Glasgow. An' Davo knows all the pigging capitals o' the world, you know? What's the capital of America, Davo?

DAVO: New York.

MACKENNA: Yer see wha' I mean? The extent of your problem, I mean. If Davo's never heard of Levington Street, how the hell d'ya expect them bastard officers? Course they gotta do more than find Levington Street, and find the Church of God. They've gotta get inside youse head. Find out what goes on . . . all those words, you know? Silent. Praying away.

MOORE: There's a church in most towns. Not just here.

[MACKENNA *sits down*]

MACKENNA: Funny that, you know. You gettin' a discharge after how long? What service you got in?

MOORE: Three months and six days.

MACKENNA: An early breakfast. I got two years and six months. And I didna bother about days. I did a year extra, you know? They put me in the Mallet for a year. But somehow they forgot to count it, you know. So am doin' three years' National Service to make up for the officer I put in hospital for three months, and six. Aye.

[*He stares at the floor.* BUCKER *and* MOORE *exchange glances.* MACKENNA *gets up, crosses to the table and puts down his mug*]

I'll tell ya what I'll do, to be fair, you know? Seeing as Mackenna canna seem ter get through to them bastard officers, and you seem ter manage it, you know? And you do three months, and I do three ruddy years. An' all for a church we all know doesna even exist, you know.

[*His hand rests on the stove*]

Stove's goin' out. Davo, warm it up. Get some coke on.

[*He moves back to* MOORE *as* DAVO *obeys*]

I'd like ter give youse a chance to prove about this church, you know? No' like them bastard officers. We'll give youse a chance, eh?

[*He picks up the crucifix*]

Now—kneel down. I said kneel!

[MOORE *hesitates and kneels*]

Facing me, you louse, me! Turn round. Tha's better. You know funny 'bout this crucifix. There's no weepin' Jesus, an' it's no' made o' wood.

MOORE: It's plastic.

MACKENNA: Plastic? Crucifix made o' plastic? Dead weird one, that!

MOORE: It's what it stands for.

MACKENNA: Huh?

MOORE: It's what it represents. That's what matters.

MACKENNA: You still believe, tellin' me all tha' crap. Aye, but I thought a crucifix was fer—hangin' people you know? Crucifixion. How the hell could you hang anybody—nail him ter plastic, eh? 'Course, if they hadna any wood in them days, they'd have had ter find another way. How's tha' fire goin'?

DAVO: All right.

[*Suddenly* MOORE *looks in horror towards* DAVO *and the coke stove*]

MACKENNA: Plastic. Would you credit it? Now what happened ta that Peter. What did he do?

[MOORE *drags his horrified gaze from the coke stove back to* MACKENNA]

Eh? Peter! That Saint, you know! What did he do, when that cock crowed thrice? What did he do?

MOORE: He denied Christ three times.

MACKENNA: Aw well! You've nothin' ter worry youse. Passed youse first test eh? We'll have youse away ter yer Church of God before that cock's even up in the mornin'. But, er, Peter . . . Didna they get him, you know? In the end. Look at me, not him. Davo's a twit. Do you fancy him?

MOORE: Please let me go.

[*Eyes closed, he mutters a prayer*]

MACKENNA: Eh now . . .

[MACKENNA *bends and kneels beside him*]

Am givin' youse a chance ter prove . . .

[*He stares at the open doors of the stove*]

No' like them officers, you know? But a' think that's right.
Ter be a priest you should have ter prove you're ready ter
die on the cross.

[MOORE *turns his head in fear at the stove*]

Or stand the flames in hell.

[MACKENNA *nods to* DAVO *and* BUCKER. *They hesitate slightly,
then quickly seize* MOORE *and force him towards the stove.*
MACKENNA *nods briefly upwards. The three men lift* MOORE
bodily on to the stove; MACKENNA *swiftly takes the laces from a
nearby army boot, and ties* MOORE's *hands behind the chimney,
speaking as he does so—*]

Yer should be able to stand the flames of hell—

[MACKENNA *pulls tightly on a knot*]

If yer can see God . . . as bright, you know . . . and glorious
. . . and Mary . . .

[MOORE *stares in bewilderment and fear, partly paralysed by the
pain*]

You can allus rise again, and live fer ever more at the right
hand of God the Father. Come again to judge the living
and the dead.

[MACKENNA *stands free and looks up at* MOORE]

MACKENNA: Forgiveness of sins . . . life everlasting. [*Soft*] That's all if youse believe. An if youse believe, youse have ter know—know there's no God. [*Slowly, deliberately*] You tell me there's no God, an' yer a free man.

[MACKENNA *stares at* MOORE. BUCKER *and* DAVO *look up in fear.* MOORE *suddenly lifts up his head in an awful inspired realisation. Then* MACKENNA *moves to sit at the table. He looks up at* MOORE, *who is staring upwards, mouth open.*

MACKENNA, DAVO *and* BUCKER *start to play pontoon.* MOORE *stands on the stove, his back curved concave as he tries to avoid burning his back. His breath is short and intermittent.* DAVO *deals nervously, one card to* BUCKER, *his hand poised to deal to* MACKENNA]

MACKENNA: You paralysed?

[DAVO *deals him a card and one to himself.* BUCKER *stares at the table as if a solution to a great problem lies there.* MACKENNA *shoves a penny forward.* DAVO *deals a card to* BUCKER, *one to* MACKENNA *and pauses before his own first card. He stares at* MOORE]

MACKENNA: And one to you.

DAVO: Mack?

MACKENNA: A card!

[DAVO *deals himself a card*]

Bucker! Call! Call, you twit!

BUCKER: Er . . . stick—

[MACKENNA *grabs his hand and forces the cards face upwards*]

MACKENNA: You canna stick on fifteen! How many more bastard times! Twist him.

[DAVO *deals* BUCKER *a card face upwards*]

MACKENNA: Six . . . lucky bastard! Fer that, I'll take half yer winnings. Now . . . [*Looks at his own cards*] A' think—

[MOORE *groans*]

I think I'll stick. Aye . . . stick. Now we wait fer the flamin' banker. Wassup wi' youse! Come on!

DAVO: He'll . . . he'll . . . Mack?

MACKENNA: Aw, are youse still—

[MOORE *cries out.*

DAVO *stands instinctively.*

MACKENNA *stares hard at his cards*]

He's frying his flamin' self. All he's gotta do is . . .

[MOORE *cries again, a long-drawn moan*]

DAVO: Mack, you can't let him . . . We'll be—

MACKENNA: Sit down, you git. He's working his ticket. A' he's gotta do is say he's working his sodden ticket. His own flamin' fault . . .

[MACKENNA'*s hand jerks out and turns* DAVO'*s cards over*]

Seventeen . . . Bank pays . . .

[*He takes a penny for himself and slides one to* BUCKER.

MOORE *is moaning continually now.* DAVO *can stand no more. He rises suddenly and goes to him*]

DAVO: Am sorry Mack . . . but . . . Christ . . . [*Sobbing*] You can't . . . Jesus . . . All right kid . . . I'll have you . . . I've got you . . . All right . . . You're all right . . . now . . .

[MACKENNA's *fist is clenched tight, his face stiff and ugly*]

[*Blackout*]

SCENE 2: *The Barrack Room. Later.*

Silence.
MACKENNA *lies on his bed, hands behind his head, staring into space.*
MOORE *sits on the edge of his bed, naked except for pants. A blanket is draped round his shoulders.*
BUCKER *stands at the table, his hand on the table edge. He stares down at it, a fixed expression midway between embarrassment and bewilderment.*
The door opens and SECOND LIEUTENANT AUDEN, *grammar-school, newly commissioned, enters and stands in the shadow.*
BUCKER *lets his hand drop to his side as he stands at attention*

DAVO [*muttering*]: Over there, sir.

[LIEUTENANT AUDEN *crosses warily past* BUCKER. *He stops at* MACKENNA]

AUDEN: You . . . on your feet!

[MACKENNA *pauses long enough to meet his gaze and then gets slowly to his feet.*

AUDEN *hesitates and goes to* MOORE *who stands awkwardly*]

B

Sit down.

[MOORE *sits again*]

What's happened?

MACKENNA: He got burned.

[AUDEN *turns*]

AUDEN: Who are you? Come here!

[MACKENNA *goes up to* AUDEN. AUDEN *senses* MACKENNA'S *menace.* MACKENNA *meets his eyes*]

MACKENNA: Two two seven nine zero zero five Private Joseph T. Mackenna . . . *sir.*

AUDEN: Mackenna . . .

MACKENNA: Aye . . . You're new round here aren't you sir?

AUDEN: I . . . was recently posted here, yes. Now what's happened to him? Let me look . . . take that . . .

[*He removes the blanket and peers at* MOORE's *wrists*]

Good God! Where else? Anywhere?

[MOORE *turns slightly*]

Hell . . . you need treatment. Anybody fetched the MI orderly? Where else are you burned? Anywhere?

[MOORE *mutters something*]

What?

MOORE: Feet sir.

AUDEN: Well, let's look.

[*He bends down as* MOORE *stretches his legs*]

Hellsbells!

[*He thinks quickly as he stands up*]

He'll have to get treatment right away. Were you here, Mackenna?

MACKENNA: No, I come in. They say he tripped and fell on the stove, you know.

AUDEN [*to* MOORE]: Did you?

MACKENNA: That's wha' he told me.

AUDEN: I'm talking to him—what's your name?

MOORE: Moore, sir.

AUDEN: Did you fall on the stove?

MOORE: No sir.

AUDEN: Then how did you get these burns on your wrists, back . . . feet? Did somebody make you stand on that stove?

MOORE: Yes sir.

AUDEN: Who?

[MACKENNA *stares hard at* MOORE, *who meets him*]

MOORE: The devil . . . tempted me . . .

AUDEN: The what?

MACKENNA: He's a religious maniac, sir.

AUDEN: Will you shut up, Mack—

MACKENNA: Here, look youse—

[MACKENNA *crosses quickly and picks up the crucifix*]

Prayin' ter it a' night.

AUDEN [*Pause*]: Are you the laddy who's applied for a discharge?

MOORE: Yes sir.

AUDEN: Mackenna, put that down and go to the MI room and fetch the orderly. Tell him it's for burns.

[MACKENNA *puts the cross down, pauses a moment, and goes out*]

Now then, let's get to the bottom. [*To* BUCKER] Who are you?

BUCKER: Bucker, sir.

AUDEN: Right, Bucker, I want the truth. Nobody's going to get hurt if we find the truth.

BUCKER: Like Mackenna said, sir—

AUDEN: Oh come on man! He didn't fall against any stove! Burns on his back and feet! He was tied to that stove! Hands behind the chimney! Obvious! I'm not a bloody idiot! Davidson, you came to me and said somebody was burnt in Holding Platoon. You were obviously here when it happened.

DAVO: I wasn't exactly here.

AUDEN: Moore . . . listen. Mackenna can't hurt you any more. If he did this, he'll get . . . well he won't be around to bother you for the rest of your service, do you understand?

[*He straightens up, disgusted*]

For God's sake! You can't let him get away with it! I've heard about Mackenna, I'm not stupid! But you can't just . . . What's the matter with all of you!

[*Blackout*]

SCENE 3: *The Barrack Room. An hour later.*

MACKENNA *lies on his bed smoking a cigarette.* MACKENNA *focuses his eyes on some remote object; his facial muscles tight, he narrows his eyes.* BUCKER *is reading a comic with concentration.* DAVO *is nervously polishing his best boots. He huffs on the high sheen and buffs them with a rag, swallows hard and glances across at* MACKENNA.

The hut door opens.

BUCKER *and* DAVO *stand to attention.* MACKENNA *waits the obligatory insolent pause before getting up.*

AUDEN *comes to stand in the middle of the room.*

AUDEN: Moore's going to hospital for a check up. They'll want to know what happened. All right, so Moore's a nutter . . . he stood on that stove to prove his faith . . . or perhaps work his ticket. Still would take a lot of guts. Don't suppose any of us here would have the same courage. What about you, Mackenna?

MACKENNA: Courage? Wha's that?

AUDEN: Guts.

MACKENNA: Oh them. A' sometimes get a pain there when on the ale, you know.

AUDEN: The guts I mean are what it takes to stand on that stove . . . like Moore. You couldn't do it.

MACKENNA: Aye, an' you're dead right, sir. I'm no' stupid, wha'ever else.

AUDEN: No, of course it would be stupid. Bravery is always stupid to people who can't manage it themselves.

MACKENNA: Wha's that for, standin' on tha' stove, if no' stupid? Stupid for anybody, eh? What point's in that?

AUDEN: Probably none, because you've nothing to prove, have you?

MACKENNA: Prove? Prove what?

AUDEN: You don't have to prove your guts . . . courage . . . Because you don't care what people think about you.

MACKENNA: Aye, that's about it.

AUDEN: Hmm. Perhaps one day somebody may be brave or stupid enough to prove you're not worth caring about.

MACKENNA [*Pause*]: Stupid.

[MACKENNA *stares unflinchingly at* AUDEN]

Ask Bucker . . . Davidson . . . sir.

[AUDEN *holds his gaze a moment then looks about*]

AUDEN: This room's filthy. I want it cleaned. I'll be back later.

[*He goes out. They watch him go. The door shuts behind him.* MACKENNA *pauses then goes to lie on his bed.* DAVO *hesitates, then goes back to his boots*]

BUCKER [*grin*]: You fixed him, Mack.

MACKENNA [*quiet*]: Bog off. Get out, both of youse. Leave me alone. [*Trace of despair*] Go to the Naafi. Jus' leave me alone, will yer?

[BUCKER *and* DAVO *move towards the door. As they reach it, it opens;* MOORE *enters, his feet bandaged and in soft slippers.* BUCKER *and* DAVO *look at him, and at* MACKENNA, *and leave quickly.*
MOORE *shuffles slowly to his locker, takes out his small pack and hesitates as he looks at* MACKENNA.]

MACKENNA *hardly reacts.*
MOORE *collects his toilet articles and puts them in the small pack.*
He straps the pack together and is ready to depart.
He stares across the poor light at MACKENNA]

MOORE: I'm sorry.

[MACKENNA *moves his head*]

MACKENNA: Eh?

MOORE: I said I'm sorry.

MACKENNA: [*Pause*] Wha' for?

MOORE: I didn't mean . . . it's not your fault.

[MACKENNA *peers at* MOORE]

MACKENNA: Wha' d'ya mean, it's no' ma fault?

MOORE: I mean . . . if you promise not to hurt me . . . not to
. . . I want to explain.

[MACKENNA *narrows his eyes, then relaxes*]

MACKENNA: You couldna explain a pigging thing, cos you're
a weak bastard.

[*No reaction from* MOORE. MACKENNA *tightens up*]

You heard wha' I said! You're a . . .

MOORE: You're not responsible!

MACKENNA [*Pause*]: I'm no' what?

MOORE: Really . . . I should in a way be grateful to you. I
mean it.

MACKENNA: What youse goin' on about?

MOORE: Well, I know for certain . . .

MACKENNA: Eh? Come here. Come where I can see you . . .

[MOORE *limps to stand near* MACKENNA]

You know what?

MOORE: That . . . I have a vocation . . .

MACKENNA [*slow*]: If youse weren't so bad, I'd kick you through that window . . .

MOORE: Why don't you let anybody . . . Look, I know how you feel, but—

MACKENNA: What you mean, you know how I feel?

MOORE: You hate me.

MACKENNA: Aye, I'll give you that. So what can you explain, eh, soldier?

MOORE: You hate me, but you didn't . . . I didn't get burnt because of you.

MACKENNA: Who?

MOORE: Me.

[MACKENNA *pauses, then grins quickly*]

MACKENNA: I dinna worry youse got bloody burnt. So youse don't feel sorry fer me? Nobody feels sorry for Mackenna, you know?

MOORE: I'm only sorry. I'm not pitying you or anything. I'm just sorry they'll blame you . . . If I had been pretending, I couldn't have stood it, could I? But I was being asked to deny our Lord . . . but you didn't know that . . . that's not why you did it . . .

MACKENNA: Oh, that's no' why I did it? You tell me, priest, why I did it then.

MOORE [*without conviction*]: You've done two and a half years' National Service . . .

MACKENNA: Aye, well, that was the justice bit. Fair, eh? Was there any other reason? Eh?

MOORE: You hate God. [*He clenches his fist in a gesture of self-control*] I wasn't going to say that. Sorry.

MACKENNA: Eh? What's all this about 'sorry'? Stop bein' sorry all over. Now what kind of God was I hatin'? Shall I tell youse? I was burning that idea, you know? You using that idea to work your ticket.

MOORE: You still think I'm lying.

MACKENNA: Well, what else you know, when there's no God! Eh?

MOORE: You're a Catholic.

MACKENNA: Who told you I'm a—

MOORE: You said part of the Creed.

MACKENNA: Oh aye, so I did. That's only ter keep off Church Parades, you know. Skive. Got to keep pretending, you know, like you. I'm no' scared o' God. Cos there isna one —right?

MOORE: But you're frightened there might be. That's what you hate, really.

MACKENNA: A' right.

[*He gets off the bed*]

I'll tell youse what I hate. I hate you, for a start. I hate your soft white skin. I hate the way you talk. Soft. An' your soft face . . . an' your hands . . . like a girl's . . . you know? I hate you and your paradin' of your God! I gotta pain down here! I hate you!

[MOORE *closes his eyes in prayer*]

I hate you, an' that's all that matters to me. An' you hate me, but you have no guts ter say it!

MOORE: I don't hate you.

MACKENNA: You said . . . in front of that bastard officer . . . you looked at me an' said I was the devil!

MOORE: I didn't!

MACKENNA: You piggin' well did! You looked at me . . . all sweetness to darkness. You said the devil was tempting youse.

MOORE: The devil inside me . . . tempting me to deny God.

MACKENNA: Oh, he's in you! Sure he's no' in me? Me, Mackenna?

MOORE: A devil isn't just one person. Nobody is completely evil.

MACKENNA: There's no devil. Right? You've said it.

MOORE: I don't think . . .

MACKENNA: There's no devil so there's no God! An' if there's no God, youse workin' youse ticket! [*He chuckles harshly*] An' you stand there tellin' me 'sorry'. An' if you're right, yer send me ter everlasting hellfire! Eh? Is that it? Aye. It's a good job we know you're a flamin' liar.

[MOORE *closes his eyes*]

MOORE: Sweet Jesus . . . I don't want to leave Mackenna torturing himself. Please help me to show him . . .

MACKENNA: Shut your flamin' trap! All right! You asked for it!

[*He goes to the stove and yanks out the poker. He brings it and whips it in front of* MOORE'*s face*]

[*Breathing hard*] Now you look at that. That's real hell fire. Now I'm going ter give you a last chance. Count three, an' you tell me that you're a stinkin' liar! Nobody gets Mackenna.

[MOORE *closes his eyes tight. He is rigid, motionless*]

One . . . two . . .

[*The poker, white hot, is a fraction away from* MOORE'*s cheek.* MACKENNA *is trembling. Suddenly he hurls the poker at the stove*]

A' right.

[*He leaps on the stove*]

I'll show you. You reckon God stood up here with you! Eh? Right. I'll prove to you . . . an' it's hot . . . it's hotter than when you . . . you time me! You had five minutes . . . I'll do six! I'll prove . . . I'll burn just to prove . . . not to get out of the bloody Army . . . But nobody beats Mackenna . . . You got your watch!

[*Suddenly the heat reaches through the soles of his canvas shoes. He shrieks in pain*]

Ah!

MOORE: Please! There's no need! You don't have to—

MACKENNA: Now you shut yours . . . an' time me . . . you know . . . Because . . . I'll prove ter you there wasna God against me . . . Now it's just you an' me . . . an' I'll show you who can take it. A minute gone? . . . Must be a minute . . .

[MACKENNA *writhes in agony.* DAVO *enters. He stops short.* MACKENNA *has his back to him*]

Who's that? [*In a voice strangled with pain*] Is that our wee officer? All right. You asked for it! . . . I'm doin' it . . . All right? . . . Aaah!

[DAVO *silently goes out*]

Come on, you bastard! D'ye want me to fry? You tell me . . .

MOORE: Please! Please don't!

MACKENNA: Say it! [*He squirms and twists on the stove, his face distorted*]

MOORE: I can't!

MACKENNA: How long now . . . eh? Come on! Come on!

[*Sweat pours down* MACKENNA'*s cheeks. As he writhes and moans,* MOORE *watches in horror, his face ashen, his body trembling. Suddenly* MACKENNA *screams, his whole body shuddering with the suffering of his flesh.* MOORE *breaks. His hands cover his eyes. He cries out*]

MOORE: Yes! All right! There isn't any God! I'm lying!

[MACKENNA *jumps off the stove and curls into a ball of pain*]

MACKENNA: Christ!

[*He shudders and squirms as he lies on the floor. Slowly he recovers. The shuddering subsides. He looks up at* MOORE, *with a faint smile*]

You see . . . Nobody beats Mackenna . . . You know?

[*He grimaces in pain.* MOORE *looks up as* LIEUTENANT AUDEN *enters, followed by* DAVO. AUDEN *approaches* MACKENNA *and stops. He looks at* MOORE. MOORE *hesitates, and goes to pick up his small pack*]

Did what you . . . ordered me to . . . sir . . . In fronta witnesses . . .

[AUDEN *stares at* MACKENNA *in fear. He is about to reply, but stops.* MACKENNA *grins. Then his expression changes as he sees* MOORE *pick up his crucifix. With his small pack slung over his shoulder,* MOORE *goes out*]

Now . . . you heard him say he was workin' his ticket in fronta me, sir. That right? I mean . . . you wouldn't want ter be . . . courtmartialled . . . fer orderin' me on ter that stove? . . . Between me and you . . . we'll come to some arrangement . . . Cos no bastard beats Mackenna . . .

[AUDEN *follows his gaze towards the exit*]

No bastard, I tell you. No bastard beats me. Me—Mackenna!

THE END

Tie Up the Ballcock

CHARLES WOOD

CAST

MR CARVER
CHATS HARRIS
MR TOOLE
GIRL
BOY
CASUALTY
BESSIE
ALEXANDRA
GINGER
RESCUE TEAM

Tie Up the Ballcock

SCENE: *The site of a Defence Exercise.*
A crushed dwelling house. Behind it is another crushed dwelling house, greyer in tone, and behind, another crushed dwelling house and another and another. Scaffolding and duckboards are twisted to form a gigantic climbing frame in front of the dwelling house. Bricks and sacking and mattresses form a burrowing at the foot of the dwelling house.
The sound of a siren. Against the crushed dwelling house are seen figures in steel helmets and overalls, armed with shovels and ropes and stretchers.
Enter MR CARVER *smiling gently at the antics of his team.*

MR CARVER: The finest body of men I ever commanded!

[MR CARVER *is in full uniform of Civil Defence officer.* CHATS HARRIS *brings the rescue team up to attention. He salutes* MR CARVER *who ignores him and shakes hands with* MR TOOLE, *saying as an aside through his megaphone*]

MR CARVER: Mr Toole is a local government official with two children and a very charming wife. How glad we are you could come. What is it, Mr Harris? Can't you see I'm talking to Mr Toole who is a local . . . Right, pay attention! You'll find in this unframed house . . . What do I mean 'unframed'?

CHATS HARRIS: A house in which the floors and roof are supported by the walls.

MR TOOLE: By the walls.

MR CARVER: That's right, Mr Toole.

CHATS HARRIS: *Were* supported . . .

MR CARVER: You'll find in this unframed house every feature of a recently bombed house you are likely to encounter. Now. Take it as read there has been an occurrence: atomic, biological, chemical. The first thing?

CHATS HARRIS: Tie up the ballcock.

MR TOOLE: Tie up the ballcock?

MR CARVER: Quite wrong, Mr Harris. Yes, Mr Toole?

MR TOOLE: Paste over the windows with brown paper.

MR CARVER: Not quite, Mr Toole. The first thing you would do?

[*A* GIRL *answers out of the rubble*]

GIRL: I should think you'd cry, wouldn't you?

BOY: Why would you cry?

GIRL: Yes. Happiness—wouldn't you?

BOY: Getting out?

GIRL: That's it. Hysterical at your release. Aftermath. Nerves would give in, wouldn't they?

BOY: I'm not going to.

[*They are lying in the rubble in a void caused by the flip-flop shatter of a floor. He has a large beam across his legs. She is in a similar predicament. Only it's across her backside. They look like they're having a picnic. Ribbons in her hair. He is in a shirt and jeans and leaning back on his elbows. Both have wounds simulated on their faces*]

MR CARVER: First thing: casualties . . . Listen for casualties.

[*A* CASUALTY *that we can't see moans*]

[MR CARVER *leans to the front, forward, his right ear cupped in his right hand, a silhouette. The team do likewise. Another moan heard*]

BOY: Was that you?

GIRL: Here.

BOY: No—I was going to say . . .

GIRL: I thought it was you.

BOY: Like hell.

GIRL: I'm unconscious.

BOY: You can let out a moan when you're unconscious.

GIRL: Can you?

BOY: Our dad does.

GIRL: Right then. Aaaaaaaaaaaaaaaaaah.

[*Which becomes a giggle for them both.* MR CARVER *taps a piece of piping with his axe handle. Clunk. Clunk*]

MR CARVER: Complete silence, please. [*Again through a megaphone—very loud*] Complete silence, please. Now then . . .

[*Selecting a* TEAM MEMBER]

Now then—it's up to you, Mr Toole.

[*With self-conscious look at the audience,* MR TOOLE *says*]

MR TOOLE: Is anyone there—can you hear me?

MR CARVER: Is anyone there—can you hear him?

GIRL: Shall I?

BOY: Up to you, isn't it?

GIRL: No—you do it.

MR CARVER: Is anyone there? How do you hear me?

[*The* CASUALTY *moans*]

MR CARVER: A reply! Yes—a reply. Yes, that was a reply.

[*March music. Enter Welfare cooks* BESSIE *and* ALEXANDRA *carrying dixies of soup to the field kitchen oven constructed in the field with no materials other than those found on the site, and lit with one match. They put the dixies down by the gently smoking oven—a thin puff of curling smoke . . . and* BESSIE, *big and Bristol, bangs on the lid with a ladle*]

BESSIE: Grub up!

ALEXANDRA: Soup up!

MR CARVER: Complete silence, please.

MR TOOLE: Well, I heard a reply—I'm sure I heard a casualty moan.

MR CARVER: Complete silence, please.

MR TOOLE [*whispering*]: From here it did sound like a reply.

BESSIE: That's all right, isn't it? Always the first thing, I always thought—it's the first thing you do—grub up. You're glad of it, aren't you? . . . that's it!

[*She bangs her soup ladle down*]

ALEXANDRA: I'd have thought so.

[*They sit—sulking*]

BESSIE: That's it then. They can get on without it!

[*They sit down—sulking*]

GINGER: Is anyone there—canst hear I?

MR CARVER: Now listen . . .

[*They do*]

MR CARVER: I shall tap again. Reply by tapping if you are able to do so.

[*Clunk. Clunk*]

GIRL: Does he mean us? Are we supposed to?

BOY: If you like.

GIRL: Was that you?

BOY: No.

GIRL: It was, you touched my hair.

BOY: It wasn't. Go on—tap if you want to.

GIRL: Why do you come?

BOY: It's only my second.

[*Clunk. Clunk*]

GIRL: And mine.

BOY: I'd rather go out.

GIRL: Do you go out a lot . . . ?

BOY: No—but I don't stop in . . .

GIRL: And me.

[*In answer to* MR CARVER's *tapping:*]

CASUALTY: Aaaaaaaaaaaaaaaaaaaaaaah.

GIRL: Should I tap?

BOY: Why do you come then?

GIRL: Why do you?

CASUALTY: Aaaaaaaaaaaaaaaaaaaaaaah.

[*Delight from* RESCUE TEAM]

MR CARVER: Right, steady on, old chap. Most likely places?

CHATS HARRIS: Fireplace?

MR TOOLE: Fireplace.

MR CARVER: That's right, Mr Toole and . . . ?

CHATS HARRIS: Spaces and cupboards under stairs?

MR TOOLE: Spaces and cupboards under stairs.

MR CARVER: Right, Mr Toole. And . . . ?

GINGER: Is anyone there—dost hear I?

CHATS HARRIS: Voids under floors?

MR TOOLE: Voids under floors.

MR CARVER: Dead right, Mr Toole. Right.

GINGER: I'm shouting my head off—why canst thee not hear I?

MR CARVER: The warden reports three occupants—right?—no surface casualties.

CHATS HARRIS: Right.

CASUALTY: Aaaaaaaaaaaaaaaaaaaaaaah.

MR CARVER: Hold on.

MR TOOLE: Bear up.

CHATS HARRIS: On our way—we *will* reach you.

GINGER: Hullo?

[*Welfare cook* BESSIE *sets her beret straight and tries again. She bangs with her ladle*]

BESSIE: Soup up. It's getting cold, see.

BOY: I'll get you some.

GIRL: I like tomato.

BOY: Won't be that.

GIRL: How will you go?

BOY: Easy.

GIRL: What will I say if they find us? Where will I say you are?

BOY: Do you want some?

GIRL: I don't mind.

[*The* BOY *pushes the beam on his legs*]

GIRL: You'll cop it.

BOY: Like to see it.

GIRL: You'll cop it—you're supposed to have burns and fractures . . . both.

BOY: That's it.

[*The* BOY *holds his elbow with one hand and swings his arm limp*]

BOY: There. How's that then!

[*The* GIRL *laughs. And the* BOY *plays fractures-hanging-limp with his leg. The same. Then he nips down the front of the bombed house and goes to the kitchen*]

BOY: What you got?

BESSIE: Now then. You a casualty?

BOY: Soup?

ALEXANDRA: Soup up!

BOY: That's it then. Twice.

BESSIE: Always ask if it's a stomach wound.

ALEXANDRA: I nearly always do.

BOY: Do I look like a stomach wound?

BESSIE: That's the first thing—I always think that's the first thing.

ALEXANDRA: 'Course it is.

BESSIE: Stomach wound?

BOY: That's it.

BESSIE: I had a stomach in the blitz. I asked him: he said 'Water'. I said 'No'. More than my job's worth to give water with a stomach . . .

ALEXANDRA [*acting*]: 'Water.'

BESSIE: 'No.'

ALEXANDRA: 'I must have water.'

BESSIE: 'No—I cannot do it.'

ALEXANDRA: How did you know?

BESSIE: You could see.

ALEXANDRA: Did he die . . . ?

BOY [*singing*]: 'My old man's in Rescue. He wears a white R on his hat.'

BESSIE: They won't tell you . . .

ALEXANDRA: I expect he died.

BOY: 'He rescued ten thousand stomachs. And what do you think of that?'

BESSIE: He had to die.

ALEXANDRA: Water.

BOY: 'One lay here—one lay there. One lay round the corner . . . One poor soul with a bullet up his hole crying out for water.'

BESSIE: More than my job's worth.

ALEXANDRA: You had to tell him.

BESSIE: He had to die. You could see that without knowing.

ALEXANDRA: Water.

BOY: 'Water. The water came at last. You can take your bleeding water and give it to the bible class.'

BESSIE: He had his legs wrapped round his neck.

[*She laughs*]

It wasn't very funny at the time.

ALEXANDRA: You have to laugh though.

BESSIE: He had to die. I told him—it's not me . . . if it was left to me you could have all the water you want.

ALEXANDRA: It's comical now.

BESSIE: You know where the grub is then my dear, don't you?

ALEXANDRA: And one piece of bread.

BESSIE: Get it down you—ought to be good.

BOY: Can I have some for someone else?

BESSIE: Not really, my love.

ALEXANDRA: See—it's not us.

BESSIE: More than my job's worth you see, my dear. He'll have to come himself. He wouldn't have you if there was an incident now, would he? Where is he?

BOY: With me.

BESSIE: You tell him to come round and he can have some— might be a stomach, see.

ALEXANDRA: That's internal, is'n' it?

BESSIE: Might make him ill you see . . . See what I mean, my love?—only it's not me.

[*The* RESCUE TEAM *are burrowing through the rubble.* GINGER *stays up top. The others can be seen twisting in and out working hard. Bits of debris fly past* GINGER's *head. Buckets full of debris are passed*]

CHATS HARRIS: Slide—can you? Look, slide up with me and get this huge segment of timber off my back.

MR CARVER: Note the timber has been charred one side.

CHATS HARRIS: I noted that.

MR TOOLE: It's been charred one side.

MR CARVER: Well done—and that means?

CHATS HARRIS: Fire?

MR TOOLE: Fire.

MR CARVER: Well . . . warm . . . but . . .

CHATS: Hiroshima . . . no—I mean . . .

MR TOOLE: Heat flash.

CHATS: That's it—I meant that . . . I was thinking of Hiroshima photographs with the shadows?

MR CARVER: That's right, Mr Toole.

BOY: Here, Ginge . . .

[*He calls up to* GINGER *on the scaffolding*]

GINGER: All right?

BOY: Dig deep.

GINGER: And you.

[*The women laugh.* GINGER *laughs and the* BOY *goes back to the* GIRL]

BESSIE: That's it, Ginge . . . dig deep.

GINGER: Full house.

ALEXANDRA: That's the ideal.

[CHATS *doesn't laugh. And when the others have stopped laughing he complains*]

CHATS: Look—all well and fine. Can you get some bod to slide up with me and get this huge piece . . .

GINGER: Dig deep.

[*A brick thrown up by* MR TOOLE *doesn't hit him—but it might have done*]

Steady on!

MR CARVER: Right. Mr Toole—perhaps I can ask you to slide up with Chats here and get this huge segment of timber off his back ...

MR TOOLE: Right. Only hold on though while I get this huge portion of concrete ...

MR CARVER: Right ...

[*The* CASUALTY *moans*]

MR CARVER: We *will* find you—Bite the bullet, old chap.

MR TOOLE: Out of my range of vision ...

GINGER: Here—I just seen the casualty—right as ninepence!

MR CARVER: Do you need assistance, Mr Toole? Right. Look, Chats—Mr Harris—can you budge back a mile and assist Mr Toole to get this huge portion of reinforced concrete out of his range ...

GINGER: Here—I knows where he's to ...

CHATS: Look, skipper—can you get Mr Toole to slide up—adjacent sort of style ... ?

CASUALTY: Please, please—I can't get out!

[*This startles them a bit—for a moment. It suddenly is obvious that the hidden casualty is a person. But only for a moment—they're laughing again soon*]

BESSIE: That's right—I can take your soup off the hot then ...

[*Laughs all round*]

BOY [*drinking soup*]: It's not bad.

GIRL: Just let me dip some bread in, that's all.

BOY: Here—have this—I'll wipe the spoon.

GIRL: No—you have it. You gave me the bread. I'll just dip some bread in . . . all right?

BOY: Are you sure?

GIRL: Yes, honestly.

BOY: Not bad is it?

BESSIE: Shut it up then—keep it warm.

ALEXANDRA: It was just he was listening. Mr Carver, see . . . he was.

BESSIE: They'll be glad of it.

ALEXANDRA: I was named after the princess—Princess Alexandra.

BESSIE: Why were you named after the princess? Why?

ALEXANDRA: Well, I've always thought it my duty to do what I can . . . it's always been my one thought, sort of thing.

BESSIE: Because you were named after the princess?

ALEXANDRA: I thought it my duty.

[*A brick does hit* GINGER]

GINGER: Here, that's not on!

CHATS: Now then, Mr Toole—together Two-six.

MR TOOLE: Two-six!

GINGER: I'm up here.

MR TOOLE: Right. Can you hang on, Two-six old chap, while I get this spiral-like twist of steel pushed . . .

MR CARVER: Bloody BLAST.

[*As the twist of steel reaches him*]

BESSIE: Are we downhearted?

[*Peal upon peal of pealing laughter from our* BRISTOL BESSIE *and her mate* ALEXANDRA]

GINGER: That just missed I. Well—don't want to make a casualty out of I . . . !

CASUALTY: Ooooooooooooooooooooooooh the pain!

MR CARVER: Steady old chap. Look . . . right . . . can you budge up a bit and get this spiral-like twist of steel out of my crutch—pardon my French—no—see it's caught round my overall and it's screwing up . . .

MR TOOLE: Right.

MR CARVER: . . . up to my matrimonial prospects.

MR TOOLE: Can you sort of bend up? Sort of bend?

CHATS: Let me take this out of your way.

MR TOOLE: Now, skipper—if you can sort of—now if you can . . . that's it.

MR CARVER: Oooooooooooooooooooooh bloody blast.

MR TOOLE: Oh dear, oh dear.

MR CARVER: I think you're hurting me actually. Can you sort of ease it? Ease it . . . ooooo . . .

CHATS: There.

MR CARVER: Thank you—thank you, Mr Toole.

MR TOOLE: That's all right. Now look—can you sort of get this spiral twist of steel out of my trouser leg . . . ? Only I don't want to cut the leg—I can't quite reach it in this position . . .

CASUALTY: Oh my God—God.

[*Sobbing and hard breath. Red pain. Red lights*]

MR CARVER: Now that's enough of that, old chap—we're trying to reach you.

BESSIE: I don't like that sort of thing—not even in jest.

ALEXANDRA: No—I'm sorry.

BESSIE: I don't like it and there's no point in my pretending I do.

ALEXANDRA: 'I'm in pain, terrible pain.' You don't care when you're in pain—just say the first thing as comes into your head.

BESSIE: I knows about pain. I see pain running down the street of . . .

ALEXANDRA: You would say anything wouldn't you?

BESSIE: Let me finish. I see pain, running down the streets of Park Street . . . I seen the whole of Bristol from Redland, all of it burning—there was pain. And the smell . . . a black greasy smell. My husband used to say—frying tonight! No, it wasn't comical at the time. We didn't find that sort of calling on our maker necessary—not at the height of the blitz.

[*The GIRL laughs. A beautiful tinkling clear laugh*]

GIRL: Did he see you?

BOY: Waved.

GIRL: What did he say then?

BOY: I said—'dig deep'.

GIRL: Was he digging?

BOY: 'Dig deep.' [*He shouts*]

GIRL: Are we deep?

BOY: He's real Bristol too . . .

GIRL: Am I blushing?

BOY: Ginge up there—he's real Bristol.

GIRL: Am I blushing?

BOY: No—you're not blushing.

GIRL: I am. I shall blush at my wedding.

BOY: What you got to blush for . . . ?

GIRL: I don't know—I just do.

BOY: I first saw you at our sister's wedding.

GIRL: Yes. Didn't she look lovely?

BOY: All right. He's a good lad . . . got a Norton 500.

GIRL: I thought she looked lovely. I shall blush at my wedding.

[*They are near the* CASUALTY]

CASUALTY: Now then . . .

[*Says the* CASUALTY . . . *very charming, frightening the* GIRL]

Now then—I can't get out. Please, oh, please, I can't get out. Can you get me out, please, please, please—if you can get me out . . .

[*A shriek of sobbing pleading. It begins to get dark quick. Smoke from the field kitchen belches. Red pain light*]

GIRL: Hold my hand. Hold my hand.

BOY: I've got it—yes.

GIRL: I know I'm silly.

BOY: I've got it.

GIRL: It's horrible—isn't it horrible?

CASUALTY: I'm burned. I'M BURNED. My eyes are burned. I AM BURNED IN MY EYES.

MR TOOLE: Bite the bullet then—there's a good chap.

[*The* RESCUE PARTY *dig on in the semi-darkness. Chink Chink —metal on stone*]

GIRL: Have you got my hand?

BOY: Yes—I'm holding it.

GIRL: I can't feel you holding it.

BOY: Yes—I'm holding it.

GIRL: They'll find us, won't they?

BOY: We'll get out—I can get out.

GIRL: No we won't.

CASUALTY: Now then, now then, now then, now then.

BOY: We can always get out.

C

[*Silence. Blackness. Silence. Digging.* BESSIE *and* ALEXANDRA *come to the front in a surprise pink spot to do a double act*]

BESSIE: Didst hear the one about the doctor?

ALEXANDRA: The doctor?

BESSIE: The doctor. And this young woman? Blonde—most glamorous. Went to this doctor one day.

[ALEXANDRA *squeezes herself into this young woman—most glamorous—blonde*]

BESSIE: 'Please, doctor—it's my hair.' 'Oh yes, young woman?' 'It's falling out.' 'Oh yes, young woman—take all your clothes off and lie down on that couch.'

ALEXANDRA: Did he?

BESSIE: He did.

ALEXANDRA: We were riding on a tumultuous sea and the waves were tumultuous high and they swept beating on the shore leaving us breathless shaken quivered spent sated ...

BESSIE: 'Come back tomorrow.'

ALEXANDRA: 'What about my hair?'

BESSIE: 'Don't worry about that, young woman. It's happening to everyone ... It's the bomb.'

ALEXANDRA: Oh yes?

BESSIE: Next day her teeth started falling out ... So she took herself back to this doctor. 'Oh yes, young woman?'

ALEXANDRA: 'Please doctor—it's my teeth.'

BESSIE: 'Oh yes, young woman?'

ALEXANDRA: 'They're falling out.'

BESSIE: 'Oh yes, young woman—take off your clothes and lie down on that couch.'

ALEXANDRA: He did?

BESSIE: Did he!

ALEXANDRA: We were flying over high mountains on a blown high tumultuous white cloud and we dropped straight shattered spent naked without breath . . .

BESSIE: Tomorrow.

[ALEXANDRA *pulls on her clothes*]

ALEXANDRA: 'My teeth.'

BESSIE: 'Don't worry about that, young woman—it's happening to everyone . . . it's the bomb.'

ALEXANDRA: Tomorrow.

BESSIE: Next day her sickness started—all green stuff.

[ALEXANDRA *mimes taking off her clothes to herself—introspective strip-tease*]

BESSIE: 'Please, doctor—it's my stomach that's disordered.'

ALEXANDRA: 'I can't stop being sick.'

BESSIE: 'Oh yes, young woman—take off your lace and your bikini nicks, young woman, and lie down on that couch . . .'

ALEXANDRA: Did he?

BESSIE: Oh yes—he did.

ALEXANDRA: We were held still—black still the air we turned

leafed in my white naked body paper from a roof—
sideslipped tumbled, locked together in grip over and over
to lie spent all spent sated cool . . .

BESSIE: Drop in tomorrow.

ALEXANDRA: Sickness?

[*Clothes on—fast*]

BESSIE: All of us—it's the bomb . . . ?

ALEXANDRA: Next day.

BESSIE: Come back tomorrow. So this very pretty woman
girl went and the very next day her skin started . . .

ALEXANDRA: Oh yes?

[*She strips again—slow*]

Peeling?

BESSIE: . . . falling—dropping from her bones all pus.

ALEXANDRA: 'Uuuuuuuuuuuuuuuuuuh. Doctor.'

BESSIE: 'Take off your scanties and lie down on that couch . . .'

ALEXANDRA: Did he?

BESSIE: No. He didn't fancy her!

[BESSIE *laughs, laughs, laughs.* ALEXANDRA *laughs and puts her
clothes back on. Back to the field kitchen, laughing*]

BESSIE: No—no. . . . Soup up?

No—soup up.

[*Cold light on the* RESCUE TEAM. *Heavy and hard breathing—
scraping*]

CHATS: Up.

MR CARVER: Back.

GINGER: Right.

MR CARVER: Now—hands.

GINGER: Here—it's a bastard, innit . . . ?

CHATS: Close-packed bastard innit?

GINGER: This aren't rescue . . . this is labouring.

MR TOOLE: Ban the bomb.

MR CARVER: That's right, Mr Toole.

GIRL: I know it's silly.

BOY: I don't mind.

GIRL: I'm glad he's stopped.

BOY: Most like snuffed it.

GIRL: What's it mean?

BOY: Dead.

GIRL: That's not funny.

BOY: No—but it's likely—way he was shouting the odds.

GIRL: Don't touch me now. Wipe that off your face!

BOY: What's that?

GIRL: That on your face—what's it meant to be?

BOY: Radiation burn. Radioactive?

GIRL: That's not funny.

BOY: What about yours then?

GIRL I want to get out—if I don't get out now I shall most likely die because I can't breathe in air. It's sitting tired on my shoulders this scream. I shall most like scream.

BOY: They'll have us out . . .

GIRL: No—I want to get out.

BOY: You must stay with me.

GIRL: I'd like to, honestly.

BOY: It's all right. I'll hold your hand.

GIRL: No—don't touch me. I can't get out—get this off.

[*She wriggles to get out—the boy tries to hold her*]

BOY: No, no. Steady on.

GIRL: Please, please—get me out! DON'T TOUCH ME!

CHATS: Belt up will you—silly cow.

GINGER: Why don't she belt up?

MR CARVER: Steady on. We *are* trying to reach you.

BOY: Don't.

[*The* GIRL *is sobbing, hunched up in her hands. She looks at the boy in the red pain light. He leans over to touch her again*]

GIRL: Don't touch me with that face—that's horrible, your face . . .

BOY: It's only bread, plastic, and red stuff.

GIRL: It's not.

BOY: It is.

GIRL: It's real—and mine is too. It's growing.

BOY: Look—it's only a mock-up burn—I wouldn't have a real burn. You haven't got a real burn.

GIRL: I can feel it's real.

BOY: Mine's not real.

GIRL: Then have a real one.

[*She deliberately scratches his face with her nails . . . looks at the resultant mess as it bleeds. And screams. But no sound*]

BOY: I'm hurt. You've got blood.

GIRL: Scratch mine—scratch mine.

BOY: No—you've hurt me.

GIRL: I've scratched blood.

BOY: It hurts.

[*Soft tears from the* BOY]

GIRL: I'm sorry . . . let me kiss it better for you—There. That better?

[*She kisses him gently*]

CASUALTY: Aaaaaaaaaaaaaaaaaaaaaaah—Jesus!

[*Darkness and red pain light*]

[*The* BOY *is not sure that he's all right*]

BOY: I'm not coming again.

GIRL: No—nor me.

BOY: I'm cold.

GIRL: Come on—let's not stay any more.

BOY: No. Right.

GIRL: Help me.

BOY: Yes. Just wait until I gets this heavy large and most likely oak beam off my legs . . . Tight. It's gripping me tight. Tight.

[*The* BOY *can't release his legs. Red lights spin as he wriggles and slaps the beam with his hands*]

GIRL: Help me.

BOY: I'm trying—I'm trying . . .

GIRL: Please . . .

BOY: I can't get out.

CASUALTY: Please, please—please, please—please please.

BOY: Wrap up wrap up wrap up.

GIRL: Please, please . . .

CHATS: Now then . . .

[*They are found by the* RESCUE TEAM. *Heads cram the entrance to their hole. The* TEAM *relax*]

GINGER: All right, now.

MR CARVER: Soon have you out.

MR TOOLE: Bite the bullet—there's good chaps.

MR CARVER: Stretchers, Mr Toole.

MR TOOLE: Right, skipper.

GIRL: Thank you, thank you. I thought you'd never come . . .

BOY: I can't get out.

[*Another surge of panic*]

MR CARVER: Soon have you out.

GIRL: Well, I'm very grateful.

BOY: Have a rest. You must be shagged out.

MR CARVER: Well—I wouldn't mind a rest.

BOY: Blokes like you deserve a medal.

GIRL: I'm very grateful.

CHATS: You seen anything of another casualty?

BOY: No—I can't say I have.

GIRL: What's he look like?

CASUALTY: Please, please. I can't get out.

GINGER: That's him . . . when I gets at him I'll pull him out of his misery.

GIRL: He got on my wick.

GINGER: You aren't the only one, my dear.

CHATS: And me.

MR CARVER: Fag then, Chats?

CHATS: I don't mind if I do then, skip.

GINGER: Smoking heavy then?

MR CARVER: Did he say something?

CHATS: I dunno, skip—I didn't hear him.

GINGER: Oh arrrrr!

MR CARVER: Like a fag, Ginge?

GINGER: I'll smoke my own—sod you!

CHATS: Don't get niggled now.

MR CARVER: No—it doesn't help to have you shouting and bawling when we're doing our level best to reach a casualty.

BOY: I should say not.

GIRL: Well, you don't want it, do you?

CHATS: That's right, my dear.

MR CARVER: See, it's a difficult job we've got at the best of times ... See—there will be survivors ...

BOY: He makes it worse, doesn't he—shouting and bawling the odds.

GINGER: He's always the same though—en he?

CHATS: Always goes too far—you know what I mean?

MR CARVER: Well—if you see him . . . you'll let us know, won't you?

CHATS: You can't miss him. He goes in for realism sort of thing ...

GINGER: Burns.

CHATS: I swear he burns himself on purpose.

MR CARVER: Looks as if he's had a quick roast in the oven of a Sunday ...

GINGER: Makes I want to throw up.

MR CARVER: If he should come while we're talking—you will let us know, won't you?

CHATS: Shout 'Casualty'—all right?

BOY: Certainly.

[MR CARVER *calls to* TOOLE]

MR CARVER: Finished those stretchers now, Mr Toole? Don't let him see you smoking—all right?

CHATS: All right, skip!

MR CARVER: He's from the Council, see?

GINGER: Bloody useless—I doesn't care where he's from.

CHATS: Soon came out when the heavy work started, didn't he?

MR CARVER: I expects he's going to be a scientific officer, see?

GINGER: Oh ar.

MR CARVER: Two blankets, Mr Toole—all right?

[*The* CASUALTY *appears behind* GINGER. *It touches* CHATS *on the shoulder. When the* CASUALTY *appears we hear Geiger-counter noises. He is covered with a white sheet and in a green spot. The* BOY *and* GIRL *shout that the* CASUALTY *is behind. They point and yell and point. No sound*]

BOY & GIRL: There he is . . . there's the Casualty! There he is . . . come on, there he is . . . !

MR CARVER: Where?

BOY & GIRL: Behind you.

MR CARVER: Behind me?

[MR CARVER *turns round right—sees no casualty. The* BOY *and* GIRL *shout and scream and shout and yell without noise*]

CASUALTY: An H-bomb explosion creates a huge white-hot fireball which last for about twenty seconds. The heat is so intense that it can kill people in the open up to several miles away.

[CHATS *takes the* CASUALTY's *hand off his shoulder and puts it in his pocket. He looks at the hand and slowly turns to see the* CASUALTY *standing there. He scampers away away away . . . knocking off the chimney of the field kitchen, and smoke starts to fill the stage*]

CASUALTY: Please please please help me.

[*He puts his other hand on* GINGER's *shoulder*]

CASUALTY: The heat is so intense it could also burn exposed skin very much further away.

[GINGER *brushes the hand to the floor, it lies there.* GINGER *stares at it, and turns to see the* CASUALTY *behind him. Exit* GINGER *into the heart of the debris*]

CASUALTY: Please, please—I'm burned.

[MR CARVER *in a low voice, behind his hand*]

MR CARVER: Did you hear the rather prime story about the tart who woke up one day to find her hair falling out?

BOY & GIRL: He's behind you—behind you . . . !

MR CARVER: Oh yes, well, she went to this quack.

BOY & GIRL: Look behind you!

[*His* TEAM *desert him, one by one as they see the* CASUALTY. *They are lost in debris*]

BOY & GIRL: No—behind you . . . !

MR CARVER: Tell me if he comes, won't you?

[*Then he sniffs. And looks sick . . . He looks at the* BOY *and* GIRL *who are still pointing and yelling soundlessly. Slowly he turns . . . sees the* CASUALTY *and runs like the clappers. Smoke has now begun to fill the stage. The* BOY *and* GIRL *start a low keening.* MR TOOLE *is folding blankets over stretchers. The* CASUALTY *stands behind* BESSIE]

BESSIE: Are you a stomach? More than my job's worth to give you anything if you're a stomach.

[*Slowly she turns and drops the ladle. Mouth open in terror, she clambers for the safety of the collapsed house and into it, heels up*]

CASUALTY: Fall-out is the dust that is sucked up from the ground by the explosion of an H bomb and made radio-active in the rising *fireball* . . .

MR TOOLE: Do not look at the flash.

CASUALTY: Exposure to radiation can cause sickness or death.

MR TOOLE: Keep food covered. Do you know that rather nice story about the young lady who found her crowning glory falling out—it appears she went to . . .

[*Slowly he turns. Exit* MR TOOLE *into the ruins*]

MR TOOLE: Don't touch me.

[ALEXANDRA *sits in the swirling smoke. She stands up and comes over to the* CASUALTY *who is moaning softly with the* BOY *and* GIRL. *She looks at him and starts to strip to grind music*]

CASUALTY: 'Oh yes, young woman?'

ALEXANDRA: 'Please, doctor, it's my mind, my mind . . .'

CASUALTY: 'Oh yes, young woman. Take all your clothes off and lie down on that couch.'

[*The* CASUALTY *starts to walk towards the stripping* ALEXANDRA. ALEXANDRA *stops. She looks at the softly moaning white thing. And screams aloud*]

ALEXANDRA: I don't fancy you.

[*Curtain and siren sounding 'all clear'*]

[*Enter* MR CARVER *in front of the curtain. He draws it back and taps the ground with the butt of his pickaxe, saying*]

MR CARVER: Complete silence, please. Hello, is there anyone there? Can you hear me?

[*Exit* MR CARVER *into the ruins*]

THE END

A Hot Godly Wind

CHARLES DYER

CAST

HARRY, *the Mediocre*
GEORGE, *the Old-or-Defunct*
POSTMAN, *who disagrees*
ERIC, *the perfectionist*
TOM, *an Everyday Ram*
CHARLIE, *on behalf of Them*
OFFICE GIRLS

DEDICATION
For my sons,
John, Peter and Timothy

A Hot Godly Wind

SCENE: *A Building Site somewhere.*
Gnarled old GEORGE *sits beside a Hole in the ground. This hole is represented by a square of black cloth surrounded by rickety barricades.* HARRY *enters merrily, with shouldered spade and pickaxe.*

HARRY: A wondrous thought contentment is. A precious atmosphere. Yet such it is. And sought by all—um, I've lost it. Gone! A wondrous thought contentment is. A precious atmosphere. By hell, it's a plush day, George! Eh, George!

GEORGE: You've taken a long elevenses: nearer thirteenses.

HARRY: Thisbe on his wild what'sit, his willow in his hand—um, that one's gone, too. So Dick the Shepherd blows his nose; and Greasy Joe doth blow his top! Ooogh, look at that Hole! What completeness! What muniference!

GEORGE: Three yobbos tried to pinch it.

HARRY: You put a cork in 'em, though, eh George?

GEORGE: Yus. Pow! Pow! Pow! That's how I went.

HARRY: Ah, me old fossil! The belly muscles ripplin'; the ancient snarlin' loins; the tautened flanks and britlin' grey.

GEORGE: I've downed a few in my time, Harry.

HARRY: Have you, George? Yobbos, pints or women?

GEORGE: Caw! Plenty of each, I'll tell you!

HARRY: That's my old mate! Ah, consider yon meticulous Hole! You what! Such aperture of cubic essence; such yawning chasm of delight. This Hole; this Pit; this Orifice.

GEORGE: They'll elect you, Harry; have you in one o' them conservatories-like.

HARRY: 'Toires, George.

GEORGE: Laurel leaf at the Eisteddyfot.

HARRY: 'Ervatoire, George; not 'ervatory. You stuff plants in 'ervatories. 'Ervatoires're where you stuff fiddlers. See, George? 'Toire as in, um—conservatoire, repertoire, and um—

GEORGE: —Lavatoire.

HARRY: I thank you. Here's me, clamberin' above my swirling pit; raising me baleful orbs in pathetic snatch at beauty; then along comes his eminence, Pope George, with his shrunken gums, withered hunkers, and his vulgar lavatoire. 'Tis fearsome wretched.

[HARRY *spits on his hands; peers into the Hole*]

Now then! Four more feet 'n I'm down to twenty-five. At what fateful spot shall I direct me spade o' destiny? A wretched problemistic nonplusment, it is! Chewable word, wretched. Wretched. It sort of chuff-chuffs round your chops, George, and tickles the der-der-ders. Wretched. Think I'll use it for a couple o' days. I'd fancy trying 'inconfutable' on somebody, too. Oh, a tittilitious sound, George. And who could I try 'peremptorous' on? Dog-mastic, it means. Peremptorous! Oh, it fondles your lips, don't you think? Eh, George? Peremptorous.

[GEORGE *spits on the ground*]

GEORGE: Yakkh! Ah, better out than in.

HARRY: Oh, I'm wretched wasted, me! A fragile petal traversin' this inconfutable sewer. Well, now—

[HARRY *gets to his hands and knees to study his excavation.* GEORGE *bends, grunting, and peers into the Hole beside him*]

GEORGE: You'll need more shorin'.

HARRY: Four be twos?

GEORGE: Six be fours.

HARRY: Shame about my failure. [*He nods at the Hole*]

GEORGE: Yus.

HARRY: Tell you another funny thing—

GEORGE: —Another?

HARRY: Ever think how lucky it is, that the holes in your face come right opposite your eyes?

GEORGE: Got one of your days, Harry, haven't you!

HARRY: I woke up with a kind of malcontent, George-me-old-sage. You see, I need to know more; and think more; but there's tickling wrinkles tellin' me I can't. Haven't the giblets up top, see? Arthritis on violins, that's me!

GEORGE: Thought you was reasonable merry first thing.

HARRY: False front, George. I'm pushing it for convenience: for convenience of you, and Them, and life. False front, George. No, I'm somewhat malcontent, George. Everythin' sounds jagged to me ear. I mean, *that* sounds jagged, George.

GEORGE: What's jagged, then? I mean, what?

HARRY: Saying 'malcontent, George'. Malcontent-Harry, malcontent-Harry. Now I'd have that.

GEORGE: What's the use calling me Harry when I'm George, Harry?

HARRY: 'Cos it lacks grace, ending my poetic observances with a stark puddingy George. Better if I was George and you was Harry, George. A George sounds better down holes than an 'Arry does. Yes! It's George goes down holes; and Harry stays up top—on his horse.

GEORGE: I'd be younger if I was Harry. And you'd be old, Harry.

HARRY: No, I'd be old-George.

GEORGE: Reckon I'd like that for a bit.

[*After a pause*]

HARRY: I shouldn't. Hate it, I would!

[HARRY *sits, hugging his knees*]

We've reached a culmination of our debate, George: potent as new genetics and metaphysicals, mate! Tell us what it's like, reaching the end of your protein chain.

GEORGE: Me what, Harry?

HARRY: Being so near death.

GEORGE: I'm not *that* bad, Harry.

HARRY: You're over the brink, though, George; so what's it like? What's it like—travellin' towards that eternal tunnel from which no tourist returns?

GEORGE: I get me twinges; and me tubes kick up, y'know, Harry.

HARRY: But your mind, George! Your mind! What's tick-ticking at this exact second in that old old noddle, eh?

GEORGE: Um—ham and lettuce for lunch.

HARRY: Gawd! Life, with food as your sole entertainment! Ancient trousers creaking to the toilet. And dead men's greenhouses—aw, they depress me wretched.

GEORGE: Don't fancy bein' George, then, Harry?

HARRY: No, I'm feeling better, George. There!—better-George flows nicer than better-'Arry. Better-'Arry sounds like an Irish bog.

[HARRY *eases on to his hands and knees; peers into the Hole*]

Someone's nudgin' our minds, George. Something very very deep's happening to us.

[*A* POSTMAN *passes by; he returns to peer over the shoulders of the two crouching men*]

POSTMAN: That's not so deep.

HARRY: You've fifteen metres there, mate.

POSTMAN: I've seen deeper.

HARRY: Why're you coming the peremptorious, mate? Postmen are friendly folk.

POSTMAN: Always smiling. The happy rat-atat.

HARRY: Laughing bicycles and rosy cheeks.

GEORGE: Householders're pleasant with you, mate.

POSTMAN: I'm forever bringing 'em things, that's why. So they smile. Because it suits 'em. Well, hard luck!

HARRY: This is inconfutably a bellicosy Postman.

POSTMAN: What am I, a mirror? A mirror, am I? Got to be nice 'cos everyone's nice to me? Are my principles any different, whether I smile or scowl? No! Nor my God, nor my mind, nor my thoughts!—they all stay the same. S'only people's reactions're different; and up the pole, the lot of 'em!

HARRY: I think he has something among there, George.

POSTMAN: What is a nice person, anyhow? He's just someone who agrees with you. Show me a nice person, I show you footprints all over his face.

HARRY: I reckon he's my other alto, George. He's dead right.

POSTMAN: Oh belt up! Don't want you agreeing with me. The only man I respect hides behind his curtain shrieking abuse at me. I love that man; can't wait to ring his bell.

[*He points into the Hole*]

What's that?

HARRY: Ah.

[*He scrambles to his feet, dusting his trousers*]

POSTMAN: Seems a shade nasty, that does, I must say.

HARRY: Sub strata, mate. Somewhere in the Macedon Era, I should hesitate a calculation; not that I'm expert.

GEORGE: Harry was hopin' to find, um, you know, like um—

HARRY: —Relics. Sub stratum delectus. Oh, inconfutably. I anticipated at least a psythian colstron deposit of some calcifected medlandromiads; but wretchedly, alas!

GEORGE: He's been quite hung-up, haven't you, Harry?

HARRY: Sic transport, George. Sic transport.

POSTMAN: It has an ominous quality: a creeping sensation.

[*They all peer into the Hole.* ERIC *enters, carrying a small cloth bag; wearing a cap. He joins the group; and peers down the Hole*]

HARRY: Them sides was plumb true; me shorin' square to a thou'; then I was flummoxed in me quest for perfection.

ERIC: Hey, what's that? [*He points*]

HARRY: That's what flummoxed me, mate. This is It. *It*, mate! My failure.

GEORGE: Oh, I dunno. [*He spits on the ground*] Yakkh! Better out than—

HARRY: —Don't clobber me principles with reasonableness, George! I crave no mitigation. That there—is my failure.

ERIC: Ah, but who sent you down there? Didn't They send you down? They carry the can, brother; not you.

HARRY: This is my job, mate.

ERIC: Oh dear! Where've you been since eternity? It's an old-fashioned yesterday when children fell from the womb with spades in their hands. Ah, a mouldy lot you are!— the old spitting father, and you, and this postman.

[ERIC *moves to the front of the Hole; he sets his cap on the ground, then produces a trumpet from the cloth bag*]

HARRY: Gaw! We've collected a ripe crustaceous congregation, George! 'Ere—!

[*He moves round to* ERIC]

What's this, then? What's the percussion lark?

ERIC: A genuine enquiry, is it?

HARRY: You're not going to play it?

ERIC: Not brewin' tea in it.

HARRY: I know your face, don't I?

ERIC: Must've been born lucky.

HARRY: Aren't you a brickie from Site Three?

ERIC: Congratulations, boyo!

[ERIC *pulls a piece of cardboard from his pocket, upon which is chalked:*

UNEMPLOYED
WIFE & 3 INFANTS

And he sets it beside his cap on the ground]

HARRY: Unemployed! But you've got a job.

ERIC: Not as a trumpeter, I haven't.

HARRY: Well, why aren't you layin' bricks, then?

ERIC: We're all Out, brother.

HARRY: We're not Out, are we, George?

GEORGE: Not so's you'd notice.

HARRY: Why's your lot Out, then?

ERIC: For better conditions, brother; and more music.

[ERIC *exercises the valves on his trumpet; then puffs a trial note or two*]

HARRY: Gaw! He'll have the fox through. Aw, this is our

pitch, mate. Me and George's and Tom's. We get our little giggle of admiring office girls come lunchtime.

ERIC: Plenty to go round, boyo. Touch of *Liebestraum* be rather tasty with this Hole of yours.

HARRY: No. Trumpet off to Site Three, mate. You're waterin' the juice.

ERIC: Talk about dogs! You have rats in your manger, brother. And us missing the light on Site Three: everythin' dark from the shade of your cancerous offices. I need the sun, brother. And thinking room.

GEORGE: Bit o' *Liebestraum* mightn't come amiss, Harry.

HARRY: Gaw! It's a ripe intervention. And catch our bellicosy Postman!

[*The* POSTMAN *is sitting on a box, unwrapping sandwiches. Now he munches one*]

Comfy, are we? Mm? Comfy?

POSTMAN: I shouldn't grumble; but I no doubt shall. I was up at five. This is nearly my supper.

ERIC: Interested in our battles of life, Postman?

POSTMAN: In peeping under the smiles, yes; peeling aside perfidious layers. Sharp healthy squabbles!—love to hear 'em. Like you and him. Truth versus mediocrity.

HARRY: 'Ere! Who's which?

POSTMAN: Shan't know till the end. [*Offering his sandwiches*] Lobster paste, anyone?

GEORGE: Yus. [*Takes a sandwich*] Ta, Guv,

HARRY: Perfidious. Smoo-ooth, is that! I can use perfidious.

[*Young* TOM *arrives, carrying a small plank. He drops it, exhausted*]

TOM: Phew! Caw!

HARRY: Whacked by a plank that size? I'd've borne a dozen at your age. On me head, African-wise: like them Bant-eye women.

GEORGE: What's up, Tom? Been on the nest, lad?

TOM: Caw! I met a shinin' woman last night. A bit old; but her energy—! Caw! And her vibration! Caw! Wild space, that woman! Real wild space. Schwoooogh! And a glow came spiralling—like, sort of—what's that kind of glow?

POSTMAN: Iridescent?

HARRY: Iridescent, that's useful. Iridescent.

TOM: Hello, darlin's!

[TOM *gesticulates at passing* OFFICE GIRLS *offstage: he minces comically*]

Pretty pretty! Hey, lovers! Can I tickle your fancy come Tuesday? Caw! Whoooogh! Hey! Back of the Post Office, eight o'clock—!

HARRY: What a ripe exhibition of delicateness and culture!

GEORGE: All blushes and flutterin' eyes in my day, it was.

ERIC: Ah yes, old father: but didn't you put knickers on piano legs, as well?

TOM: 'Ere, Harry!

HARRY: What?

TOM [*points into the Hole*]: What's that?

HARRY: Gaw! I'm conglomerated with pointin' fingers, and trumpets, and sandwiches and iridescent womanisers.

TOM: Yeah, but what is it?

[TOM *goes on all fours to peer closely down the Hole. And the others gather round to gaze, as well*]

HARRY: Why not debate the perpendicularism, the cubicness of its presence?—instead of what's-thattin' with your grubby stubs. Everybody's what's-thattin'.

GEORGE: You don't reckon it's growin' bigger, Harry?

HARRY: 'Course not! Just people getting nosier. Why can't you lot thump off?

[HARRY *picks up his spade; forces a way through the huddle*]

Thump off! Thump off! Leave a man to his labours!

ERIC: Digging more dirt, brother?

HARRY: Too true, mate.

[HARRY *is about to clamber over the barricade*]

ERIC: Not going down there, are you?

HARRY: Well, I can't dig from up here, can I!

ERIC: Oh dear, how dull you are. Edges blurred through grovelling to Them. They own you, see? Come here; dig there; sit down; jump up! And you do it. Poor brother Harry, so deeply unhappy, not knowing why.

HARRY: Oh Gaw! Give over, mate! I was smilin' 'til you lot stirred me up.

ERIC: No, Harry, no! You have niggling doubts; a scratching behind the eyes. You have, you know. Reaching for open doors, you are; and finding empty rooms.

HARRY: I struggle for perfection, yes.

ERIC: As with this Hole?

HARRY: As with that Hole, yes.

ERIC: And *that*? [*Pointing*] Is there always a *That*? Something spoiling it for you? An abstraction, and no posh word for it, save—failure?

HARRY: I told you this! In regard to our present Hole here, *that* is my failure, yes.

ERIC: But for you, Harry, everything has its failure ingredient: every hole, every day, every time. Inadequate, you are! You are inadequate, Harry-boyo! So you're unhappy. See?

GEORGE: Malcontent, he said. Malcontent—

HARRY: —Never mind! Never mind, George.

ERIC: So I'm bang on target, brother!

HARRY: I held certain metaphoric debates with George-here upon vague puzzlements of my subconscious, yes. But then, a simple nut like me must be quite iridescent to a bricklayer from Site Three. Gaw!

ERIC: It was your posh words, boyo; but you're not posh enough for the words. Did you know they were mostly misplaced and mispronounced?

[HARRY *is embarrassed; he shuffles, glancing sideways at the others*]

HARRY: Yeah, but it's only fun, isn't it. It's a satirical—a satirical thrust at—at— [*He falters into silence*]

GEORGE: —Go on, Harry! You come out with one of your, like, you know—one o' them funny witticisms, like.

HARRY: I wouldn't misdemean myself, George. Not with him!

POSTMAN: Don't let him push you under, Friend. At least, he's spitting in your face; not behind your back.

ERIC: You agree with me, Postman?

POSTMAN: It's my principle, Friend, to disagree with everyone. And you are a typical under-arm tailor.

ERIC: Me? A tailor?

POSTMAN: Under-arm. Telling your neighbours how to dress; with your own backside tattered to hell.

ERIC: Ah, but you must agree with my logic.

POSTMAN: I don't agree with you talking at all! Why not blow him a raspberry, and pass on your way?

TOM: 'Ere! You said you loved squabbles, though.

POSTMAN: Didn't say I agreed with 'em. I love oysters; but I don't agree with 'em.

ERIC: What of Truth versus Mediocrity? Are you asking me to gag the truth?

POSTMAN: Who wants truth? Nobody needs it. Too depressing. That's why I disagree with *de mortuis nil nisi bonum*.

HARRY: Gaw! That was impressive. Most impressive, that one.

POSTMAN: Never speak ill of the Dead!—I say it's the one time you should speak ill: when they're past caring! Lobster paste, anyone?

GEORGE: Ah, yus. [*Takes a sandwich*] Ta, Guv.

HARRY: Stuffin' yourself, George! You'll spoil your lunch, mate.

GEORGE: Yus; but I can only have it once.

ERIC: Complacency, that is George. Harry is Doubt. The Postman is, um—Argument. I am Truth; and Tom is—

[TOM *yells after more Girls*]

TOM: Over here, kittens! Hoy! Here, lovers, I'll tickle your fancy! Whoooogh! Cheeky-cheeky—!

HARRY: Now tell us he's deeply unhappy!

POSTMAN: And tell us *who* he is!

ERIC: Oh, Tom isn't anyone in particular. He is all of us, see? Tom is Everyman.

HARRY: There's a ripe load of—undiscernibleness.

ERIC: Not at all, boyo. It's true. Tom rises to the morning, seeking no message; grubs in the mud for sustenance; fills his belly; hugs his wench; plants his seed in lusty soil; then sleeps with the night. And providing he snores past Death, all problems are solved till tomorrow.

TOM [*at more Girls*]: Hey, Phyllis-baby! Your place tonight, love? Is your Mum out? I'll tickle your fancy. Whooooogh!

[TOM *tries an exuberant handstand; then collapses giggling to the ground, and sits rubbing his hands in glee*]

ERIC: Lust in the dust; or What the Woodworm Saw!

POSTMAN: Do we understand you are somewhere above us common throng—what's your name?

ERIC: Eric, brother. Eric. Old Scandinavian for 'Ruler'. Some of us must point the way, you see.

HARRY: Gaw! He'll crack his elbow patting his back. One thing's inconfutable, mate: you don't need a trumpet. 'Ere, George, he doesn't need a trumpet, eh?

ERIC: Same quip twice, Harry? No no no no, boyo! Where's your improvisation? You could have said, um—

[ERIC *walks round the Hole, dramatising his examples*]

—'His mouth is too big for trumpets, bring him a euphonium!' Or 'Who needs Holes with a mouth like his?' Or, here's a quickie: 'Only thing bigger than his head is his mouth. Boom-boom!' Or you could have said: 'Sing hymns, brothers, for Jesus thinks he's here!' Or how about—'Draw back the black curtains of space, this trumpeter's mouth will serve!'?

GEORGE: Nah, you couldn't beat our Harry, mate; not when he puffs his steam up. He'd show you! You show him, Harry! Make him look ridiculous!

ERIC: Alright, Harry. Match my trumpet on your triangle.

GEORGE: Say something telling, Harry-boy!

HARRY: Give over, George! I can't do it when people're watching. [*Whispers*] He's hammering me under, this bloke; screwing me into the ground.

ERIC: Destroying you, am I, boyo?

HARRY: You've ears like a bugle, too.

ERIC: That's a bit better. But there's no shame in destruction, not for you nor me-the-destroyer. From your ashes will rise a brand-new dodo. Let us christen this moment, brothers! As we stand in the presence of this, Harry's celebrated Cavity, a new dodo shall emerge from its inadequate mystery!

TOM: Never mind his trumpet: I reckon he's split his crumpet!

ERIC: Ah Tom, Tom, Tom! It is for the young to destroy all yesterday's diseases; and without mercy. For true humility is acceptance of our own inadequacy, and the need for our eventual destruction. Life itself is destruction, a shameless chain of living and dying. New ideas grow ugly and tumble into death; but from death burgeons a beautiful, exciting Progress.

HARRY: Yeah, well, just sort of grubbing my mind among your multi-coloured hogwash, mate, I'll tell you one thing: Man may have a few old-fashioned diseases, but if God has one—it's Progress, mate!

ERIC: I like it! By God, I like it! D'you hear him, Postman? George and Tom? Eh? Harry was gold-plated, there! Marvellous, boyo!

[ERIC *almost dances around* HARRY, *slapping his back and wringing his hand*]

This time you *have* had a success, brother! Say it again! Quick, quick, quick, before it vanishes.

HARRY: You mean about God having, um—

ERIC: —Don't pause, Harry-boyo! So many little words from little persons blip into space, yet no life should fade without setting its crotchet of music on history. Quick, Harry, and we'll make your crotchet a symphony.

HARRY: Oh, well, I just said that Man may have—

ERIC: —some old-fashioned diseases; but if God has one, it's Progress!

POSTMAN: Your symphony, Harry; but he finishes it!

ERIC: I'm stealing it, you mean?

POSTMAN: Too true. Be using it as your own by teatime.

ERIC: And why not? No copyright on Thought, Postman! Can't stop a man whistling, can you?

HARRY: But it's *my* thought. Gaw! Me one bit of original psychologic maxim; then up he comes and pinches it! A killing thing, that is. A killing thing.

ERIC: Ah, didn't I say life was destruction? Man is unimportant. It is the song he leaves behind; and that is for everyone. You've had your moment of glory, Harry-boyo. Be content!

HARRY: You're somewhat patronistic, aren't you, mate!

ERIC: Flesh is to the earth, brother. But music is vibration; is thought; is mind, and eternal time. Our few paltry moments until we are worm-eaten and defunct, like George, grizzling there—

GEORGE: Hey! Nah then—! Harry was at me this mornin'; and now you!

ERIC: Nothing personal, old father. Same for us all. Our allotted span is but a finger-click against eternity.

POSTMAN: And you wonder why I'm disagreeable? Why I'm all for honest-to-Godness? It's this Eric and his kind with their self-enwrapped atmospheres of government and culture; their intense dedication; their descent from dark brown to holy pink when they announce 'Thought for the Day'. *Their* thought for *their* day; but we're all expected to yessir-yessir and jump in with 'em.

[*The* POSTMAN *rises, screwing his sandwich paper. He is about to throw it into the Hole*]

D

HARRY: D'you mind!

[HARRY *grabs the crumpled paper; and pockets it*]

How would you like me stuffing rubbish into your post boxes?

POSTMAN: I take the point, Harry. I was carried away. I became enflamed in my hopes for a simple laughing life where holy thoughts fall from God—instead of Party campaign head-quarters.

ERIC: Oh, that old God! You mean the old-fashioned Spirit? The One you split into three?—and then hung on crosses and chains, and made statues of? Oh, that old myth!

POSTMAN: Is He finished, then? Is He done with?

ERIC: He had a long long long run; but did nothing for the race, brother.

POSTMAN: Mm, well, He still keeps a few people company: He's good for loneliness, you know. It's dream stuff, I admit; but it's a change from licences, and regulations, and applications, and closed shops, and false-information-given-on-this-form-renders-the-person-liable-to-blah blah blah blasted blah!

ERIC: And how about those centuries of God's closed shops? The cruelties, horrors, of Popes and their Inquisitions—?

POSTMAN: —I'm talking of today, here, now! Don't blame me for the horrible Romans. Oh, you don't understand. None of you understand. How d'you tell a jellyfish the water's cold!

ERIC: It was you mentioned God, brother; not me! Always dangerous, it is! Always dangerous! I suppose your various

Gods'd know how many archbishops they've employed; Calvinistic moderators; priests and imams from Islam to hell-and-back! But do you? D'you know how many popes you've had? Do you? Or you? Or you?

HARRY: Um, let's see now, um—

ERIC: —Six Pauls, eight Alexanders, eight Urbans, twelve Piuses, thirteen Leos and thirteen Innocents, fourteen Clements, fifteen Benedicts, sixteen Gregories, and twenty-three holy Johns! What a parade across history! What overwhelming godliness! And what a record of disaster, misery, and suffering!

POSTMAN: Always dangerous!—blaming yesterday.

ERIC: Up until this morning, we've had a calculated seven thousand nine hundred major outbreaks of war since Jesus, not including Geronimo! So what're you going to do about it? Eh? You, Harry! And you, Tom—what're you going to damn-well do about it, eh?

TOM: Yeah, but I mean, what're you shouting at me for?

ERIC: Don't you think little people have suffered enough?

HARRY: *We know they have, mate!* We're little people ourselves, aren't we? Anyhow, who put you in the chair? Casting your vitiperations at me, and Tom, and George. He's a senior citizen, is George.

GEORGE: Yus. A ripe liberty.

HARRY: Show some respect for your elders, mate! Learn by the sagaciousness of the all-encompassing wisdom of this gaffer of God's communial!

GEORGE: Yus. I've lived, I have. A packet o' years under this belt, mate.

ERIC: And it's you I blame most of all. Nothing personal, George; but old folk imbue me with such hopelessness. What they have done is forgotten; and no time for what they have in mind.

POSTMAN: George'll love you for that!

HARRY: D'you hear, George? No time for you, dad! Finished! Best climb in this Hole; I'll toss some dirt on you.

[*They laugh raucously.* HARRY *slaps* GEORGE'S *back; and* GEORGE *(seated) slaps* HARRY'S *legs.* ERIC *moves to them angrily*]

ERIC: That's how you forget! By laughing! One thing I abhor above inadequacy is the insensitivity of cow-like minds digging holes! Useless holes!

HARRY: 'Ere! You're waxing a bit personal, mate!

TOM [*clenched fists*]: Shall I duff him up, Harry?

HARRY: In a minute, Tom. Can you not comprehend, *brother*, that this Hole is but one cog; that we're all of us converging in the entirety of a mighty complex. Not just you brickies on Site Three; but all of us! There'll be a thousand offices in this block.

ERIC: What for?

HARRY: A million square feet of—what for? How d'you mean, what for?

TOM: Shall I duff him proper, Harry?

HARRY: In a minute, boy! In a minute. *What for!?*

ERIC: What for? You've housing lists long as time; families begging for homes. Why aren't you building homes?

POSTMAN: Yes, why aren't you, Harry?

HARRY: Well, I mean, they um—they um—

ERIC: They?

HARRY: Yeah, you know, um—I mean, they're not building offices for nothing, are they!

ERIC: They're building 'em for money, Harry-boyo. That's the reason. But what's the use? Ask your disagreeable Postman!

HARRY: You think offices're useful, don't you?

POSTMAN: Don't agree with offices. Two thirds of life offices're dark; folk could be sleeping in them. And every Saturday, every Sunday, offices're dead: families could be living there.

ERIC: Not forgetting those most sacred precincts, closest to God: the executive suites and directors' snogging pits which are empty ninety per cent of life. Then the gorgeous board rooms, brethren! Silk, velvet, plush and crystal—all created in the image of heaven for one day a year. *One day a year!* One day to receive a host of podgy fat bellies, grunting *Hear-Hear!* and *Motion Passed!* before tumbling tired to the golf course. The only important hole in this mighty complex is the Nineteenth.

TOM: Yeah but, I mean—'cos, like, we gotta have *some* offices, don't we?

ERIC: We've got them, Tom. Enough for forever. The cities're clogged with 'em; we can't breathe for 'em, see the sun for 'em. Offices offices offices! Let the white collars double-up or something; and for God's sake, Tom-boyo—start building homes!

[*He draws close to* TOM, *speaking urgently*]

Watch it, Tom. Watch it, boyo!—because by the time you're settled and married, even if you get a home, there'll be so many without that They—yes, *They*—will be knocking on your door, saying 'How many can you take in your kitchen?'

[ERIC *crosses to* HARRY; *and speaks close to his ear*]

A knock at the door, see, Harry; and there's the billeting inspector with his little red flag and a sad hungry queue clutching his hand. 'Now then, Harry,' he says, 'how many will your bathroom hold?' D'you fancy that, brother? Mmmm? You and the Missus?

HARRY: Gaw! And I've just done it up in instant marble.

ERIC: Ah, just the job, boyo. Posh bit o' marble! They may let you keep that, although there'll be a standardisation of decor, you see. S'only fair: why should one billetee get a better house than another. And you'll have to keep a special clean window for governmental stickers—big penalties for tearing 'em off, you know: 'This is to certify Harry's bathroom has been requisitioned for six homeless humans.' And there'll be a sensitised strip for computers; and an ominous rumble everywhere.

HARRY: Six homeless humans! You'll need a circus act. [*To* GEORGE] Or they won't half scorch their bottoms on our geyser.

[*Everyone laughs except* ERIC]

ERIC: Don't think it's not coming! It's coming alright; and I hope you're still laughing in ten million people's time. Not long, ten million. Tiny Land. And shrinking fast, it is! Soon be clogged with offices. So They will limit your gardens. No roses! Cabbages only! X yards per person; and alternate breathing! Got any roses, Harry?

HARRY: A few, yeah. I've um—got a few nice um—a few nice ramblers, yeah.

ERIC: Why should you have roses, when people are homeless?

[*A pause*]

TOM: Hasn't it gone quiet!

[ERIC *moves downstage of the Hole; sits on the ground in front of it, and polishes his trumpet*]

POSTMAN: Anyone noticed what a pendulum this Eric is? Left to right, he swings. Tick tock. Left to right.

ERIC: But which is left, Postman, and which the right?

POSTMAN: Depends on what particular They you have in mind.

ERIC: Ah, some They or other. There will always be a They; not so sure about England, but definitely They.

TOM: 'Ere—!

[*He scans the distance to left and right*]

—It *is* quiet, you know. Been no crumpet in ages! We get real zingers about now on early lunch. Whoooogh! But it's all deserted. 'Ere!—wouldn't it be great if we was really all dead round this Hole. Like on Television. You know. Sort of In-Between, waiting for our Maker. And this wheezing sort of, you know, hot godly wind'd surge upon us; and a whackin' swirlin' mist; and this old geyser with his—caw!—flowing whiskers and un-wrinkled eyes'd sort of beckon us up up up!—up these shadowy stairs to Above.

POSTMAN: More like a thumping black ladder [*he points at the Hole*]; and a whacking tongue o' flame calling us down down Below!

TOM [*impressed*]: Yeah. Caw! I wonder—?

[TOM *goes to the Hole; peers into it. The* POSTMAN *rises, and stands beside him; then* GEORGE; *and lastly,* HARRY]

ERIC [*over his shoulder to them*]: Shouldn't dig any deeper, Harry!

HARRY: Oh sure, it's all me! Tongue of flame'd be *my* fault! I reckon he'd look like me if he popped up: he'd have me father's eyes. Bloodshot eyes, me old Dad had. Oh hell!— to mint a phrase.

ERIC: So you'll down tools, then; and come Out?

HARRY: You serious?

ERIC: Certainly. Tell Them you've held useful discussions .. cautiously optimistic . . . interim settlement . . . difficulties not insuperable . . . providing they tear down these offices and build homes.

HARRY: Gaw!

ERIC: You'll come Out, won't you, Tom!

TOM: Oh. Well. I mean, 'cos like—this is your kaleidoscope, mate, isn't it. I mean, it was the old un's did it; not us young.

POSTMAN: Satisfied with your young lot? Got all you want, then?

TOM: Well, I dunno, do I! Not till I need it. 'Slike saying I'll never do it again.

GEORGE: What you done, Tom?

TOM: I haven't done nothing, George. I'm explaining an example, see! I mean, it's easy saying you'll never do it again—when you don't want to. How d'you know you won't do it again, until you feel like it? Eh?

[TOM *sees some Girls*]

Hey, Phyllis! Come on, sweetheart! Oogh, they're lovely! They're lovely! Whoooogh!

POSTMAN: Doesn't seem we're dead, after all.

HARRY: I am! And face to face with myself. Shall I tell you something? Shall I impart a most cantankerous fact? I don't know why I dug this! This Hole. They didn't tell me.

ERIC: Come to harbour, brother! You're beginning to think, Harry-boyo.

HARRY: Yeah; and the fun's gone. Must've dug a hundred holes. 'Come here! Stand up! Dig there,' they said. And I never asked why.

[CHARLIE *enters: a beefy, beaming Foreman*]

CHARLIE: Well well well well, my children! How goes the day then?

HARRY: Aw, button up, Charlie!

CHARLIE: Now then, Harry! Mustn't snarl at me! I'm your Foreman what loves you. Hee hee!

HARRY: Oh Gaw!

CHARLIE: Is Harry cut-up over something, then?

ERIC: He is disillusioned, brother; face to face with the uselessness of life.

CHARLIE: Aren't you Eric from Site Three?

ERIC: I'm here to practise my *Liebestraum*.

CHARLIE: Very nice, too. And the Postman's here to listen. Very nice. I married the Missus to *Liebestraum*. Lovely. De dah dah de dah, de dah de dah de—

HARRY: —Why're we building offices? Eh?—instead of schools, and hospitals, and flats for the homeless?

CHARLIE: Um, I wouldn't know about that, Harry.

HARRY: Then you damn well ought to, mate! A wretched Foreman, stewin' in the complacencies of his own juices. Where's the Sage pointing the way? Where're the Wise Men to save me drowning? Why don't you say something wise, you lobsided gaffer?

CHARLIE: Now, Harry, we mustn't be insubordinate, lad!

GEORGE: Didn't oughta speak to Charlie like that, Harry.

HARRY: And you, George! Hanging round my neck with your palsied eyes and grumbling stomach. Say something wise, you wrinkled bat! And young Tom, with his freaky pelvis; that bellicosy Postman and his niggling; and him! —Eric the trumpeter, stirring it up, stirring it up, stirring it up! And another thing, Charlie!

[HARRY *points into the Hole*]

HARRY: What's *that*!?

CHARLIE: Oh yes. Mm. I knew about that.

HARRY: What is it, then?

CHARLIE: Mm. Something strange there. Yes.

[*He shakes his head; in-draws his breath*]

HARRY: Don't know, do you, Charlie!

CHARLIE: No. No, I don't, Harry. No. Mm.

HARRY: And why was it dug? This Hole?

CHARLIE: Oh, I can help you there, Harry.

HARRY: You can?

CHARLIE: Oh yes. Because of Them, Harry. They wanted it dug.

HARRY: What for?

CHARLIE: To have a look at *that.*

[HARRY *covers his face with his hands; groans*]

HARRY: Round and round the deep deep Hole!

CHARLIE: They needed to inspect it, see, Harry.

HARRY: And? [*Uncovering his face*] What did they say it was?

CHARLIE: Um—they didn't seem to know. But they said it was nothing to worry about. So you can fill it in again, now.

HARRY: Gaw! Oh, Gaw—!

[HARRY *sinks to his knees; rests his head against the barricades*]

ERIC: Futility is born out of useless labour! Splendid! Full circle! [*Rubbing his hands*] You may tell your Lords, Charlie, that we have had useful discussions—

HARRY: —No, I'll speak for myself. Something I do really well. Not much to say: except the Trumpeter's right.

[HARRY *rises, speaking quietly, sincerely and humbly*]

You're right. I conceive every point. All true. No excuses. If I said I felt like, you know, creeping somewhere to weep! And I mean it!—for being, you know, inadequate, and for failure to muster my mind to the heights I dream of. Gaw, I have some secret dreams!—but I can't make the daylight catch up. You've rumbled me, Trumpeter. Fair cop! Mediocrity.

[*He pats* GEORGE's *shoulder*]

Sorry about the grumbling belly, George.

CHARLIE: Aw, very nice, Harry. Nice and human. You can get filling in now, eh?

HARRY: No, I can't.

CHARLIE: Why not?

HARRY: Lunchtime. Come on, George; Tom!

[GEORGE *and* TOM *begin collecting their spades and pickaxes*]

ERIC: You've given no answer, boyo! No answer.

HARRY: Haven't got one. I'm thinking ferociously, but—I mean, I'm no God-man myself. I'm humantist and that stuff. But I've this accumulating niggle about swapping Dying Heaven for your Trumpet.

ERIC: Not to worry, give me more time, Harry. And I'll show you how to be perfect.

HARRY: You perfect?

ERIC: In my principles, I am. Rock-hard ideals, I have. I'm confirmed, Harry.

HARRY: Mm, yes. That's my itch: tossing out me tattered

Bible and geniflexing to *Liebestraum* on the mantelpiece. 'Cos no matter how good and true, none of us is almighty, mate.

ERIC: Yes yes yes. You're right.

HARRY: We all make up God. All us people together.

ERIC: Yes yes. Absolutely right.

HARRY: —Us mediocre, us ugly, us stupid. And believe me, I'm all three; but—Gaw! I'm in a ripe mess.

[HARRY *covers his eyes; shakes his head*]

A ripe mental mess. [*Uncovers his eyes slowly*] D'you know, I think if you'd laughed a bit, I'd've been with you. But I don't remember you laughing. We're all damn fools, too; that's what makes us laugh.

ERIC: I'll remember for next time. Thank you.

HARRY: Anyhow, I'd like you to know everything you say is right, Eric. Too many offices; not enough homes. Too much God; not enough Man. Too many Rules; not enough Hope. I shall try and come up with somethin' inconfutable. I'll try. I promise.

ERIC: But that's tomorrow, brother. What of today?

HARRY: Yeah. It's been a ripe perfidious morning.

POSTMAN: I don't agree. At the very least, we're still here. What d'you expect?—Miracles? They don't shine from holes. If you need miracles, climb out and walk to Jerusalem. [*He offers a pill*] Indigestion tablet?

HARRY: Don't use 'em, thanks.

POSTMAN: See! You're one up already. Ta-ta! [*He exits*]

[HARRY *shoulders his spade and pickaxe*]

TOM: Have you ever thought about us eating sheep, Harry? I mean, 'cos like, caw!—great woolly things, sheep are; and we put 'em in our mouths; and mulch 'em.

HARRY: Not the whole sheep, Tom.

GEORGE: Yus, and they pluck 'em first.

TOM: But birds, and pigs, and eels. We shove 'em in our human mouths.

HARRY: Only after they're dead, Tom; and apportionated into palatial forkfuls.

TOM: Shoving bits o' dead fellow creatures into our stomachs. Pretty little lambs. Just think if they were still moving—

HARRY: —Urrrgh, Gaw! Trumpets and wriggling food—

[HARRY, GEORGE *and* TOM *walk off.* ERIC *is packing his trumpet*]

CHARLIE: I thought you were going to play *Liebestraum*. I could die to *Liebestraum*. 'Smy one bright spot. Aren't you going to play *Liebestraum*, then?

ERIC: No, brother. Going where there's people. Can't waste my music on futile Holes. I need to show people the way; and make them happy.

[*He exits; so does* CHARLIE . . .]

CHARLIE [*to himself*]: I'd've loved a bit of *Liebestraum*. De dah dah de dah. De dah de dah de dah dah. Dah dah de dah de dah—

THE END

Class Play

DAVID SELBOURNE

CAST

JOHN
FRED
KATE

Class Play

SCENE 1: *A school room, or school hall, or anywhere.* JOHN *and* FRED, *close together. Apart from them,* KATE. *They are all about fifteen. They all loathe the disciplines of school. They are free, to that extent. They fear the future, and do not care for it either. They are bored. They alternately like, and hate, each other. They have no hopes; nor ambitions. They are happy too, for the time being. All three are present throughout.*

JOHN: Go on, ask her!

[KATE *turns away*]

Go on!

FRED: No! Why don't you?

JOHN: You daren't.

FRED: Who says I daresn't?

JOHN: I do.

FRED: Who are you, eh?

JOHN: Me. That's who I am.

[*Silence*]

FRED: And who's that exactly? Eh?

[*Silence*]

Why should I?

JOHN: Heh–heh.
Why should you?
Because she's got you going, that's why.
You . . . like her.
Heh–heh!

FRED: You ask her then,
If you're so jeering.
You do it.
You daresn't.
Go on, big mouth.
Jeerin'.
You daresn't!

JOHN: You!
Huh!
Look at you.
She wouldn't be interested in a type like you.
What have you got to offer?

[*Silence*]

FRED: What . . . type am I then? Eh?

[*Silence*]

I got more 'n yoo!

JOHN: 'More 'n yoo'!
What a way to speak!
Learn to speak properly, pal!
Look at you!!

SCENE 2: JOHN *apart,* FRED *apart,* KATE *apart.*

FRED: John's a bastard. I don't mind 'im.
   She must be a nice girl,
   The way she does things,
   I could watch 'er all day, just breathin',
   Walkin', talkin',
   You watch 'er.
   I can't get near 'er.
   I daresn't ask 'er!
   You watch 'er now, just watch 'er.

JOHN: Nice chick, really.
   Sexy bird.
   Legs and that.
   Teasing though.
   The usual business.
   Bloody women.
   I've had enough of them.
   Waste of time.
   Money, records, dancing.
   What's the point?
   They just use you.
   Use them.
   That's my policy.
   Use them.
   I don't mind trying.
   Just to nark him.
   Bloody coward, rough-neck.
   Come out tonight,
   Eh, darling?
   When you've done your homework?
   Heh-heh!
   How about it?

KATE: I'm a virgin.
  I don't want to.
  I'm careful.
  That's all Fred's after.
  I can tell.
  The way he watches, sneaking.
  It makes me creepy.
  He just isn't open.
  He's so . . . so furtive.
  It makes you shudder.
  John's so normal, and a good talker.
  He's more cheerful.
  [*To* JOHN]: All right, then, John.
  Seven o'clock.
  At the corner.

JOHN [*to* FRED]: O.K. pal?
  How about that?
  D'you see?
  It's easy.

SCENE 3: JOHN *and* FRED, *close together.* KATE *apart.*

FRED [*looking quickly towards* KATE]: Look at 'er face!
  Why's she smilin'?
  What's she got to be so pleased at?

JOHN: Me, pal!

  [FRED *and* JOHN *look at each other, and laugh together*]

  She likes me.

She's got a secret passion.
She's got a crush on me.
Look at the way she's smiling.
Stick around, pal. Heh-heh.
I could teach you.

FRED: She doesn't mean it.

JOHN: She's got real judgment.
She's a beauty.

FRED: You're just sayin' it now.
Pretendin'. You dunno what yer sayin'.
You don't mean it!

JOHN: I mean it.
If I choose to mean it,
I mean it.

FRED: I can't keep up, mate.

[*Silence*]

What . . . are you going to . . . do then?

JOHN: Mind your bloody business.

FRED [*squaring up to* JOHN]: What are you after?

JOHN: Come off it.

FRED: She wouldn't go with a pig like you!
How could she?

[*They struggle*]

JOHN [*jeeringly*]: Take it easy, take it easy.
Behave, Fred!
Where's your manners, Fred?
Girls don't like that kind of roughness.

Be gentle. Tone up your behaviour.
Take it easy. Eh?
That's right now.
You need a few more lessons, pal. That's your trouble.

FRED: She's just a bitch, then!
I thought she was decent.
She's nothing.
I thought she was . . . was . . . I dunno.
Different.
It's 'opeless.

SCENE 4: JOHN *apart.* FRED *and* KATE, *together.*

KATE: You're just a lout.

[*A silence*]

You've got no manners.

[*A silence*]

That's the way louts talk.
You're just a lout.

FRED: I . . .

KATE: . . . You want to wash your mouth out.

FRED: I didn't mean it.

KATE: You said it, didn't you?

FRED: I didn't mean it.

KATE: Why do you say it then,
 If you didn't mean it?
 Tell us another.

[*A silence*]

FRED: I only . . . said it. I . . .

KATE: Yes, you said it.
 That's what I'm telling you.
 You said it.

FRED: What's saying?

KATE: Saying's meaning.

FRED: Sayin's only sayin'.
 It's not meanin'.
 It doesn't have to be meanin'.
 I didn't mean it.
 Did I?

KATE: How do I know?

FRED: Because I'm tellin' you.

KATE: So what?
 I don't care, anyway.

[*A silence*]

Mean it if you like.
 If you like, mean it.

FRED: I don't mean it.

[*A silence*]

I just thought . . .
 . . . I just thought you was different.

[*A pause*]

KATE: You make me sick.

FRED: I thought you wouldn't fall for it.
   I thought you was different.

KATE: John's . . . so courteous. I like him, really.

FRED: I thought you was different.

   [*A pause*]

   I . . . still do.
   Kate.

KATE: You're . . . soft.
   You are a baby,
   Aren't you?

   [*A pause*]

   [*Giggling*] What's the matter with you anyway?
   Eh?

SCENE 5: JOHN *and* FRED, *together.* KATE *apart.*

JOHN: You want more style, friend.

FRED: Where's that get you?

JOHN: Where it's got me, pal.

FRED: It's got you nowhere.

JOHN: Oh, hasn't it?
   Further than you, pal.

FRED: Don't call me pal.

JOHN: Further than you, eh?

FRED: Stop braggin'.

JOHN: Bragging, am I?
Did she say yes, or didn't she?

FRED: Don't ask me.
I dunno.

JOHN: She said yes, pal.
And you know it.
You heard.

FRED: What if she did?!
What's that to me? Eh?
Do I care?

JOHN [*taunting*]: Yes, pal, you do, don't you?
Tell us.
Go on, Fred. Tell us, Freddie.

FRED: You don't deserve it!

[*A silence*]

You don't deserve a girl like 'er.
You don't know what you're gettin'.
You don't care one way or the other.
It's nothin' to you, is it?
I can tell,
It's nothing to you, is it,
One way or the other,
Is it?
Eh?

JOHN: Don't get so excited.
  As a matter of fact,
  No,
  It's nothing to me,
  One way or the other.
  I don't give a damn,
  One way or the other.
  I'm just . . . exploring,
  One way or the other.

FRED: You're . . . you're . . . callous.

JOHN: Spell it!

FRED: You're callous.
  You're cheating.
  You're . . . abusive!

JOHN: Heh-heh.

FRED: You don't deserve it.
  She's too good for ya.

JOHN [*squaring up*]: Oh yeh?

FRED: Yeh.

  [FRED *and* JOHN *pushing each other.* KATE *tries to stop them.
  They turn their backs to her*]

JOHN: Oh yeh?

FRED: Yeh!

JOHN: Who says?

FRED: I says.

JOHN: And who are you, eh?

FRED: Me.
  That's who I am.

  [*A silence*]

KATE: John.

JOHN [*to* KATE]: You keep out of it.
  I don't want any trouble.
  So you stay out of it.
  Right?
  Get me? Get right out of it!

FRED: You want more style, friend, eh?
  Don't yer?

  [JOHN *grabs* FRED]

  Don't get so excited! Don't get so excited, mate!

  [FRED *pushes* JOHN *away*]

KATE: Fred.
  Don't, Fred.
  Please. Truly.
  For my sake.
  If only for my sake.

FRED: I'm just a lout, Kate,
  Eh?
  Aren't I?

JOHN: You said it, pal.

FRED [*shouting*]: I'm just a lout, eh,
  Aren't I?!!!

  [*A silence*]

JOHN [*to* FRED]: Shake.

[*A pause*]

It's not serious.

[*A pause*]

Come on, Fred. Let's go home.
It's not worth it.
For a bloody woman like her.
I ask you. Let's go home.

SCENE 6: JOHN *and* FRED, *together.* KATE *apart.*

KATE: Boys are so stupid.
So insensitive, really,
When you think about it.
They just want to use you.
They're so crude,
Both of them,
Really.
There's no difference between 'em.
It's so tiresome.

They've got no real feelings.
A girl's life is really lousy,
I'm telling you.
They're so dirty.
The things they get up to.

I'm a virgin.
I don't want to.
I'm thinking of the future.
I'm more mature than they are.

They're children.
Look at them.

Look at me.
I'm older, really.
I'm the same age, actually,
But I'm older, really.
We had it in biology.
It's all quite simple.
Girls are more understanding,
Thinking of the future.
Not all about our bodies,
But serious,
I mean it.

I want to have a lovely future.
This is just fooling.
They can both hang themselves,
For all I care.
I don't mind the trouble.
I quite enjoy it.
But I'm not being exploited.
I'm thinking of the future.

[*A pause*]

You can go now,
The pair of you.
I've changed my mind, John,
Actually.
I've got to wash my hair tonight, John,
Truly.
Another time, eh?
I promise,
Really.

SCENE 7: JOHN *and* FRED, *together*. KATE *apart*.

JOHN: So crude? So dirty? She's raving!

FRED: I said you didn't deserve 'er.
I told you!
Serves you bloody right.
That cocky with 'er.

[*A pause*]

That'll learn you.

JOHN: . . . Teach you.

FRED: That'll teach you.

[*A silence*]

Did you 'ear 'er talkin'?

JOHN: 'They can both hang themselves,
For all I care!'
Yeh, I heard it,
And that means you, pal,
So pipe down.

FRED: And you, mate.

JOHN: And you, pal.

FRED: She's more mature than you, mate.
You 'eard.

JOHN: Oh, yeh?

FRED: Yeh.

JOHN: And you, pal.

FRED: I got nothin' to lose.
It's you.
Where's yer seven o'clock at the corner now, eh?
I got nothing to lose.
You've got no real feelings.
I . . .

JOHN: . . . Yeh?

FRED: You . . .

JOHN: Yeh?

FRED: Spoiled it.

JOHN: Spoiled what? Eh?

FRED: For me.

JOHN: Oh yeh?

FRED: She's got sense.
She was tellin' you all that, not me, mate.
Really.

JOHN: Oh yeh?

FRED: I was watchin'.
I could 'ear it.
The way she was talkin'.
She was tellin' you.
She just . . . just didn't want to 'urt your lousy feelin's.

JOHN: Oh yeh?

FRED: So she put me in as well,
But it wasn't me, it was you,
She was tellin'.

JOHN: Oh yeh?

FRED: You ask 'er.
   Go on, then.
   Find out, mate.
   Go on, then. Please. Go on!

JOHN [*to* KATE]: Who did you . . . ?

KATE: . . . Both of you!

FRED: Kate?

KATE: And you!!

JOHN: O.K. wise guy! And you!

FRED: And me?
   I . . .

   [*A silence.* KATE *and* FRED *look at each other briefly*]

KATE [*gently*]: Boys are so stupid.

SCENE 8: JOHN *and* FRED, *close together.* KATE *apart.*

JOHN: Do you think we give a damn then?
   You and your lovely future!

   [*A raspberry*]

   She can keep it, eh Fred?
   Virgin!

   [*A raspberry*]

   No bloody wonder.
   You can keep yer lovely future.

Kids and dish-cloths,
Dusting, cooking, bingo.
You can keep it.
I can see it coming.
We've got no real feelings, have we?
More than you have,
Boys are so stupid, are they,
What about girls then?
You're not so brilliant.
Fred and me's . . . independent.
Eh, Fred?

[*A silence*]

KATE [*to* JOHN]: Where are you going to go then,
Independent?

JOHN: Get a job,
If I want it.

KATE: Oh yeh.
Where, exactly?

JOHN: Anywhere.
Any job.
No problem, eh Fred?

KATE: You'll be on your own, John, soon.
When school's over.

JOHN: Independent.

KATE: Clocking-on, beer, and swearing,
If you're lucky.
You wait.
You'll see.
You don't impress me.

E

JOHN: I thought you said I was 'courteous'.
  Didn't she Fred, eh?

[FRED *nods*]

Make your mind up!

KATE: When you're after something,
  You can seem decent.
  You know how to turn it on, that's all.
  That's different.

JOHN: Come off it.
  Tell her, Fred.
  It's no use me talking.
  She's gone all superior.
  Go on, tell her.

KATE [*to* JOHN]: Leave him alone!

[*A silence.* FRED *looks briefly at* KATE]

FRED [*to* KATE, *fiercely*]: Stop foolin' me.
  I don't need no girl's protection.
  You're just flirting me.
  You aren't serious.
  You're 'urtin'.
  You're spiteful.
  It isn't workin'.
  I'm not wearin' it!
  I'm too crude for you,
  So don't go all meltin' on me.
  'Leave him alone', eh?
  What's 'e doin' then?
  Nothin',
  Compared with your foolin',
  Provokin',

That's all you know,
Teasin', leadin',
Squeezin', squirmin'!
You need a damn good 'idin'.

JOHN: Well said, Fred.
Let's go, pal.

[FRED *pushes* JOHN *away*]

KATE: You don't mean it, Fred.
You're in a temper, aren't you?

FRED: I mean it!!

SCENE 9: JOHN *and* FRED *close together.* KATE *apart.*

JOHN: Let's go, pal.

FRED: Where?

JOHN: Out.

FRED: Where?

JOHN: Anywhere.

FRED: Where's anywhere?

JOHN: Somewhere.

FRED: Where's somewhere?

[*Both laughing*]

JOHN: Anywhere.
E*

FRED: Yeh.

JOHN: Fag?

FRED: Yeh.

[*They light up*]

JOHN: That's better. Ffff.

[*A pause*]

[*To* KATE]: Want one?

[KATE *turns her back*]

You can't tame 'em.

[*Gently to* KATE]: Go on,
I got plenty.
Plenty where that came from.
Relax you.
Let off a bit o' steam, sort of.

[JOHN *and* FRED *laugh*]

[FRED *makes as if to go towards* KATE]

[*To* FRED]: Stick with me, pal.

SCENE 10: JOHN *and* FRED, *together, backs to* KATE.

KATE: Big shots.
Kids.
Messing.
They don't know what they're saying.

They're just like children,
The pair of them.
Look at them.
They're up to something.
They don't care about people, really.
They're only interested in themselves.
They were only having me on,
In the first place.
They're not bad really.
Just a bit childish.
They just don't know what they're saying.
I could forgive them,
If they're truly sorry.
If they'd say they didn't mean it,
I could forgive them.
They wouldn't do it.
They're so pig-headed.
They just don't know what they're saying.
I kept my self-respect.
I'm not falling for their nonsense.
I told them.

[*Exit* JOHN, *jauntily, self-consciously, smoking*]

They're up to something.
I know it.

[FRED *turns tentatively to* KATE]

They're just like children,
The pair of them, you are, Fred, truly,
Kids messing,
They're not bad really,
Just a bit childish,
I could forgive them,

If they're truly sorry,
They wouldn't do it,
I'm not falling for their nonsense.

FRED: Kate.

KATE: We hurt each other,
Because we've got no future,
Nothing much to hope for, really.
It's very simple.

FRED: We've got a future.
We all 'ave.
You wait and see, girl.
We've got a future.
We all 'ave.

[*They remain apart*]

THE END

Brainscrew

HENRY LIVINGS

CAST

HARRY STEADMAN
MARY HASS
ALISDAIR MENDIP
RECORDING ENGINEER

Brainscrew

SCENE: *A Recording Studio.*
Three elegant modern chairs are set, and a table with three tiny silver microphones and a little green cue light. Water carafe and glasses on a little wooden tray, pads and pens; there is a studio clock. Meanwhile ALISDAIR MENDIP, *friendly man, comes forward to chat with us.*

ALISDAIR: Good evening, everybody, my name is Alisdair Mendip, and I'm chairman and referee of . . . 'Brainscrew'. 'Brainscrew' is a parlour game for a million and two, a kind of 'Charades' where nobody's allowed to leave the room. The rules are simple: we have two contestants.

MARY HASS *and* HARRY STEADMAN *enter casually and arrange places to suit themselves either side of the middle chair at the table; professional smiles for each other, and for us.*

ALISDAIR: I'll spin a coin, and one of them calls. Whoever wins the toss dreams up a set of circumstances, and the loser of the toss has to find out what the circumstances are. If he or she were to say 'fares please', for instance, the other contestant might suppose himself to be on a 'bus', right? No direct questions, any number of guesses, and I'm sure you'll all be guessing like mad.
Our guesser can join in and play the circumstances where he thinks he knows the way, and when he's sure he knows where he is, he says so, and the round is over.
Our contestants tonight are actress Mary Hass . . .

She inclines her charming head

ALISDAIR: . . . and journalist and scourge of pomposity and evasion in high places, Harry Steadman.

HARRY: A-vailable for Masonics and smoking concerts.

ALISDAIR: Any minute now that little green light is going to flicker, and we shall be in recording time, so can I ask you, please, *not* to call out your own guesses? And one more thing, can I ask you to be rather silly and help us with some applause at the top of the show, mm? I give a nod, and you clappa de hands, right? Just for me. I'm putting in for a higher fee tomorrow and you've no idea what a difference it'll make.

ALISDAIR *distributes that well-known smile and goes back to his place at the table.*

Bit of sotto chat.

Looks up to the wings brightly.

The cue light flickers.

ALISDAIR *nods for our applause, which is backed by recorded applause subtly over the P.A.*

The cue light goes off.

ALISDAIR: Good evening, everybody, my name is Alisdair Mendip, and I'm chairman and referee of . . . 'Brainscrew'.

Pause. Faint noise of signature tune being played in offstage.

Signature is piped into the P.A. . . . and out again for a second of offstage twitter and . . .

Cue light again

ALISDAIR: 'Brainscrew' is a parlour game for a million and two, a kind of 'Charades' where nobody's allowed to leave the room. The rules are simple: we have two contestants, I'll spin a coin, and one of them calls. Whoever wins the toss dreams up a set of circumstances, and the loser of the toss has to find out what those circumstances are.

If he or she were to say 'fares please', for instance, the other contestant might suppose himself to be on a 'bus', right? No direct questions, any number of guesses, and I'm sure you'll all be guessing like mad.

Our guesser can join in and play the circumstances where he thinks he knows the way, and when he's sure he knows where he is, he says so, and the round is over.

Our contestants tonight are actress Mary Hass . . .

She inclines her charming head.

ALISDAIR *invites our applause eagerly and with a nod and a lifting gesture of the hand, and speaks plumb into it when he's got it . . . backed as before from the P.A.*

ALISDAIR: . . . and journalist and scourge of pomposity and evasion in high places, Harry Steadman.

ALISDAIR *again invites our applause, and again it is backed,* HARRY *slipping in his witticism:*

HARRY: A-vailable for Masonics and smoking concerts.

ALISDAIR: And up goes half a crown. Mary, would you like to call?

MARY: Heads.

ALISDAIR: And . . . heads it, no it isn't, tails it is. Tails. Harry, off you go.

HARRY: Right-o. [*Moment's thought*] Henry Irving bit coming up hochachachar:

He stands and steps away from the table, mimes incompetently opening a small heavy door, and peering upwards beyond it.

MARY: Ye-es, opening a heavy door . . . a small one . . . and . . . I wonder is it significant that the door was not locked and that you didn't turn the latch . . . ?

HARRY *with hasty comic gestures ducks out of the door and slams it, naturally catching his fingers, and then elaborately turns the imaginary handle and carries on as before.*

HARRY: Doing me imaginary nut here I am.

HARRY *begins to mount spiral steps, growing progressively wearier, casting hopeful glances at* MARY *for rescue.*

MARY: It's a tower of some sort. A tower. No handrail . . .

HARRY *puts out a hand for a handrail and then changes his mind after a thought.*

MARY: Could be cut within a cliff-face, or underground . . . solid anyway . . .

HARRY *rests, puffed, looking hopefully at her. She doesn't seem enlightened, so he gestures her to follow him.*

HARRY: [*Faint . . . as if distant . . . call, through cupped hands*]: Come on . . . up!

She hurries to his side, but he shakes his head, still gasping . . . no, she's got to come up the stairs.

MARY *turns, appealing to* ALISDAIR.

MARY: Do I really have to, Alisdair?

ALISDAIR [*nods*]: You'll have to do the twirly twirly if you want to be up there with him, Mary.

MARY [*setting about it daintily, trippingly*]: Oh pish.

As she ascends, HARRY *suddenly places his hands over his ears, ducking and weaving his head as in the throes of some excruciating experience.*

MARY *arrives by his side, and watches his face excitedly for further clues.*

He releases a hand and gestures for her to also cover her ears.

MARY [*covering her ears*]: Noise! It's a noise!

HARRY *strains painfully to hear, nodding encouragement.*

MARY: A very loud noise! Yes.

She tries to get in front of him to query his face, shouting against the presumed din:

MARY: Where?

HARRY *shakes his head frantically at her movement, releasing a hand momentarily to press her back where she was, away from some appalling chasm before them, rolling his eyes down at the presumed depths.*

MARY: Waterfall! Waterfall!? Niagara?

HARRY *allows his arms to drop, and turns weary and glazed eyes uncomprehendingly to* MARY *as she shrieks:*

MARY: It's a waterfall! No? Ship's hold in a shipyard? Is it?

HARRY: What're you shouting for with your hands up to your ears?

She looks gasping giggly at the palms of her useless hands.

MARY: I shouldn't be shouting?

HARRY: I don't think so, somebody might wonder what we're up to; now that it's over.

MARY: Now what's over?

ALISDAIR [*genial but hasty*]: Ah ah Mary: no direct questions except your guess.

> HARRY *takes her hand with brave solicitude to lead her sidling away back along an imagined ledge.*

> *She gazes merrily into the chasm before them, stops, looks up at* HARRY, *who waits with that old merry twinkle for her guess.*

MARY: Heavens above, it's a belfry!

> *She throws back her head in charming glee.*

> HARRY *sparkles his assent and leads her back to the table.*

ALISDAIR [*beaming*]: Now we know where Harry's place is: the belfry. My goodness, those bells. What time was it, Harry?

HARRY: About thirty-four o'clock I think.

ALISDAIR: Well, you old campanologist.

HARRY: Beast.

ALISDAIR: It's time for you to exercise your brain, and Mary to exercise her imagination. Away you go, Mary.

> MARY, *deep thoughtful breath. Then politely and evenly businesslike, as she will be throughout, to* HARRY:

MARY: I'd like you to sit by me over here. [*To her left, slightly downstage and away from the table*]

HARRY: All right. Is that all right, Alisdair?

ALISDAIR: I think I can make it all right. . . .

HARRY *takes his chair and sits where she asked him to, while* ALISDAIR *follows him with* HARRY's *mike; takes a stand from the wings and fixes it so that* HARRY *will still be recorded, speaking into it as he goes, smoothly:*

ALISDAIR: Harry is now moving so that he's opposite Mary, instead of having me between them . . . and Mary, Mary is writing headings on her scribbling pad . . . at least . . . no, her pen seems to be retracted, so that she's *marking* the paper . . . without looking down. [*Backs hastily away back to his own mike before continuing*] Am I correct in my interpretation, Mary?

MARY *carries on marking the pad.*

HARRY: Are you acting writing? or are you . . . ? You're not particularly paying attention . . . are you doing what you seem to be doing? Coo-ee. Simply marking the paper? This is a stonewaller.

MARY: Can I have your name please?

HARRY: What's that? You . . . Ah, you *don't* know my name. I must get my brains oiled. My name is Harry Steadman.

MARY: Date of birth?

HARRY: 20.9.20. Sounds like the vital statistics of a Dutch Doll. . . .

MARY: Height?

HARRY: Five foot ten inches.

MARY: Actual?

HARRY: Actual?

MARY: With or without shoes?

HARRY: Five foot ten without with shoes. Oh I don't know. Five foot ten for heaven's sake.

MARY: Weight?

HARRY: Thirteen stone. Stripped.

MARY: Did you bring your portrait photograph with you?

HARRY: No, I . . . should I? You didn't ask. You did ask? You sent for me?

MARY: Never mind. [*She sits, still as ever*] There.

HARRY: Wassat? Did something happen? I said I haven't a photo.

MARY: Any physical peculiarities?

HARRY: Alisdair, I think I'm entitled to know what's going off? I just said I haven't a photo, and she said never mind and then . . . [*He's baffled to say what did happen*]

ALISDAIR: I think it's all right, Harry, the circumstances may well dictate Mary knows and does things you don't know about.

MARY: Physical peculiarities?

HARRY: There's sump'n sneaky goin' on round here. I have no physical peculiarities.

MARY: Colouring?

HARRY: Me? I'm red, white and blue with 'Buy British' written down my middle.

ALISDAIR: Oh come on, Harry, play up, and play the game.

HARRY: 'Ere, who's side are you on? [*Back to* MARY] Colouring? *Look* at me. I'm here. You remember me. [*Thought*] You aren't allowed to look at me? Yes. Mmm. Right: hair light brown, eyes blue. Curly eyes and light brown teeth. It's entirely my answers that count, mm?

MARY: Now would you put your hand palm down flat on this pad?

[*There is no pad*]

MARY: Yes, and now press it onto the paper. Thank you.

HARRY *virtuously follows her instructions.*

MARY: Now the other one . . .

HARRY: Each one is quite unique. Isn't that extraordinary?

MARY: Peculiar.

HARRY: Not particularly peculiar.

MARY: Not unique, peculiar.

HARRY: I think I need a moment to think that out. . . .

MARY: Your handprints are not unique.

HARRY: No, really they are.

MARY: There are copies on this paper, aren't there?

HARRY: Oh. Yes of course.

MARY: Which are peculiar to you. So far as we know.

HARRY: Yes, mm. Ha ha, some Aborigine in the desert rubbing just two such identical prints together at this moment. [*He realises he is rubbing his hands, and stops*] That'd throw you for a loop.

MARY: I don't think so.

HARRY: Yes, I see. It could just as easily be my problem. Not so good, eh?

MARY [*throwing him nothing*]: Use this cloth to wipe off the ink.

HARRY [*catching nothing*]: Yes.

MARY: Address?

HARRY [*pounce*]: You've sent for me. How could you send for me without knowing my address?

MARY: I didn't.

HARRY: So how did I get here?

MARY: You came here.

HARRY: I c . . . [*Shuts up*] Twenty-seven Penkridge Avenue, Goston, Derbyshire, England. What am I doing here?

MARY: Giving information. Uncoloured facts.

HARRY: Am I in trouble?

MARY: Not at all.

HARRY: I'm glad.

MARY: Yes.

HARRY [*bracing himself*]: What else d'you want to know then?

[*Turns to* ALISDAIR] Am I permitted to invent? For the purpose of the game?

ALISDAIR: No, I think you must stick to the truth, Harry. Only Mary may invent.

HARRY: Not even an itsy bitsy teeny little invent? We had one last week.

ALISDAIR [*avuncular*]: Only if it fits, and if Mary accepts it.

HARRY: Phew. O.K. Let's go. How's the time?

ALISDAIR *and* HARRY *glance at the studio clock, but are brought back by* MARY, *who has her own time:*

MARY: It's four-thirty, Wednesday.

HARRY: Who'd a thought.

MARY: Don't you want it to be?

HARRY: Me. I'm highly chuffed, yes. [*Sniffs a thoughtful sniff*] Four-thirty. Children'll be out of school. [*Looks at her to see if he's got the wavelength. He has*]

MARY: Who's looking after them?

HARRY: My wife'll be seeing to them. You want them in on this? Be an extra fee.

MARY: Your wife will be seeing to them. They're waiting?

HARRY: Waiting? Where? Oh, all right then, I suppose they are, somewhere or other. Who's looking after them?

MARY: They're all right; you . . .

HARRY: Are you *sure* they're all right? [*Cunning, she's not coming up with very good answers, push her for a slip*] How d'you know that?

MARY: . . . . your wife is also with them.

HARRY [*smirk*]: They're only young, can't leave them with strangers.

MARY: Your wife is also with them.

HARRY: Yes. Yes you said so. I said so. Who said that? Wanna fight? I didn't like the look of that attendant, did I?

MARY: Attendant?

HARRY: The attendant. Dammit, surely I can have one insy winsy attendant to look after my poor fatherless bairns?

ALISDAIR: Mary? Can he have an insy winsy attendant?

MARY: Your wife is also with them.

HARRY: I think I've got that. It's not necessary to keep repeating that. Can we get on?

MARY: Married?

HARRY [*explosive*]: Well for . . . ! *Yes*. Married.

MARY: Thank you.

HARRY: Don't be personal.

MARY: What?

HARRY: You said thank you. I said don't be personal.

MARY: Yes.

HARRY: Please, is this all we're to have? Just a series of trivial facts?

MARY: You consider them trivial?

HARRY: Do *you* consider them trivial?

MARY: I don't consider them at all. *When* were you married?

HARRY [*getting a bit sullen about it all*]: April the third, nineteen fif . . . nineteen forty-eight.

MARY: Children born?

HARRY: Yes.

MARY: When?

HARRY: Sorry. Girl: May thirty-first, fifty-six; boy fifty-eight.

[*Pause*] November second.

MARY: So that the girl is eleven and the boy is eight.

HARRY: When you think about it, you're not much further on for all the facts, are you? I'm completely in the dark so far . . .

ALISDAIR [*gliding in*]: I'm really puzzling here. . . .

HARRY [*not pausing*]: . . . but you, equipped with factual detail . . . it's like the human body being so many pints of water and trace element: true, but not terribly relevant . . . not a good *description*.

ALISDAIR: Harry . . .

HARRY: I mean it's not really *me*. I don't feel it's me, although I know I'm the one that's answering the questions, I know that, and of course they are about me. I once characterised a man by saying that he always seemed to have his braces so tight his feet only just reached the ground. It seemed quite adequate.

ALISDAIR: I'm sorry, Harry, but can we get back to our muttons?

ALISDAIR *glances at the clock, and* HARRY, *uncertain, follows his eye.*

The clock jerks on its way with a faint chunk chunk chunk.

HARRY [*tentative*]: This is rather like a hospital, isn't it?

MARY: Yes.

HARRY: I've had no serious illnesses. Was inoculated and immunised against malaria, yellow fever, diphtheria and smallpox in the army.

MARY: Any surgery?

HARRY: Surgery?

MARY: Any disorder requiring surgery?

HARRY: No.

MARY: Thank you.

Pause.

ALISDAIR *is about to come in, but* HARRY *fills the gap:*

HARRY: Yes, long corridors, very clean; with occasionally a streak of filth that's quite impossible to understand: how could anyone so meticulous miss it? An atmosphere of patient indifference, lonely pain, antiseptic and anaesthetic.

MARY: Yes.

HARRY: Why?

MARY: I just said you're right.

HARRY [*feels he's on the right track, and beginning to play it, the old quizzical*]: Somehow, quite irrationally, I detest those glimpses of quiet surgery, through thick glass. The still lifes of unconscious patients waiting, or busy but silent assistants swabbing tiled floors. Surgical booths. But I always have to look.

MARY: You saw surgical booths?

HARRY: Did I? Oh yes. Yes, so I did. Must have done, walking by, following the attendant. Frightening myself to death here I am.

MARY: You walked by, following the attendant?

HARRY: I didn't like the look of him. He never spoke or looked back, eh?

MARY: Yes, but the surgical booths . . . ?

HARRY: You couldn't see in.

MARY: Yes you could, you said you did.

HARRY: You're warped.

MARY: You could see in. What about the children? Did you hurry them away?

HARRY [*watching her carefully*]: As far as they were concerned . . . it was just, interesting.

MARY: The insides of people don't look distressingly ill?

HARRY: Can we finish with this? I think it's in rather poor taste.

MARY: You'd rather walk by?

HARRY: No. I said already I let the children look, out of . . . scientific interest. It's part of life. It's reassuring to them.

MARY: You reassured him?

HARRY: Who? The boy? I reassured them both, the scene reassured them. That surgery is not a personal nightmare: it's a repair job. The surgeon is a skilled man who is not interested in you, only in the facts of you . . . [*Abrupt*] Why am I here?

MARY: I told you. Facts only.

HARRY: I'm not ill, there's nothing wrong with me?

MARY: No.

HARRY: Sort of census.

She inclines her head in assent.

HARRY: Yes, yes it's a census. I expect I've seen others, neighbours, coming and going. It's not just me.

MARY: It's not relevant.

HARRY: I think it is. It matters to me. I was lonely, pig in the middle here, without the others. Everybody's just looking at you, well, you begin to wonder who it is they're all looking at, I can tell you.

MARY: All right, have it your own way.

HARRY: Eh? [*Sniffs*] Well then, that's all right.

MARY: You've seen them? From your own street?

HARRY: Avenue.

MARY: All right, avenue, the facts are yours. You've seen people brought away to here?

HARRY: Oh yes, but of course I had no idea what it was.

MARY: You didn't ask.

HARRY: Of course not. I should get a pretty short answer, I should think. 'I see you were taken away, you and your good lady, Mr Beverly. . . .'

MARY: So *someone*, some authority, assembles comprehensive

facts about everybody, and you aren't consumed with curiosity?

HARRY: I am indeed, and I'm here to find out.

MARY: *I* am here to find out.

HARRY: Look I don't want to be uncivil, but that's the sort of bloody silly repartee every civil servant can handle.

MARY: You don't want to be uncivil.

ALISDAIR, *a merry gurgle in appreciation of the exhange, as who should say 'Break!'*

ALISDAIR: Now here we are at the half-way mark, d'you want to take a guess, Harry? I think we're having a lot of fun here, or shall we change ends?

HARRY [*with a struggle for cogency*]: So it's an authority is it?

MARY: No.

HARRY: I don't know why a firm 'no' should sound so evasive.

ALISDAIR: It looks as if we're going on, folks.

MARY: Is your family still there?

HARRY: Still waiting? I suppose so, aren't they?

MARY: Go and look, the door isn't locked.

HARRY: No, why should I?

MARY: Your wife may feel that the boy has been disturbed; or maybe they got restless and naughty.

HARRY: Nonsense. Stick to your data, something you understand.

MARY: Did you tell him why you were coming here?

HARRY: I was told to.

MARY: What this place was, and why you, why *you* were compelled here, and him with you?

HARRY: You said it was everybody.

MARY: It's all right if it's everybody? Is that what you told him?

HARRY: I'm baffled to know why you harp on the boy.

MARY: Young males are more vulnerable.

HARRY: You talk like a half-baked text-book, we hardly see him.

MARY: He's very sure of you? And therefore of himself?

HARRY: Some children just are more secure.

MARY: Independent.

HARRY: Yes.

MARY: Don't need an invincible father.

HARRY: *Yes.*

MARY: What did you say when he came in the gates here? 'Don't worry'? 'Daddy won't let anything happen'? Did you catch your wife's eye and nod and smile?

HARRY: All right then, I did. Satisfied?

MARY: I'm not even interested. Now affiliations.

HARRY: You're dictating my assumed behaviour in the most ludicrous way. I'll agree, for the sake of the game; but really, it's a bit pulp-magazine. 'Turn and catch my wife's eye. Nod and smile.' Forsooth.

MARY: I didn't say anything about turning. Affiliations?

HARRY: Affiliations? What about them?

MARY: What organisations do you belong to? And what is their purpose?

HARRY [*makes a decision*]: No. Finish. I give up, I've had enough.

ALISDAIR: I don't think you can do that, Harry, your chance to do that came and went: time is our master here.

HARRY: Yes you can. Like 'I-spy'. I give up, and she gets another turn.

ALISDAIR: No: there isn't time for another turn, you see.

HARRY: It's a totalitarian state, right?

MARY: No.

HARRY: All right then, I give up, what is it?

MARY: What organisations do you belong to?

HARRY: Oh shut up. [*He stands, scraping his chair back*]

ALISDAIR: I don't understand your objections, still I suppose we must respect them.

HARRY: Not you too, Alisdair: I've given M . . . Mary best, do I have to take on you as well?

ALISDAIR: I don't follow.

HARRY: I didn't raise any objections: I gave up.

ALISDAIR: Well don't, try again.

HARRY *glances at the clock chunking on. He sits, not moving the chair back to the stand mike.*

HARRY: That clock makes a noise.

ALISDAIR [*coming over to push the mike nearer to* HARRY]: Does it? [*Listens*] Yes, I suppose it does. Could we carry on?

HARRY: I refuse to give an account of my affiliations.

MARY: Thank you.

HARRY: Wha . . . ?

ALISDAIR: Carry on, Mary. You see, Harry, all you have to do is respond to the circumstances. 'Yes' or 'no' or 'I won't' will do as well as anything. You refuse to say what organisations you belong to, right, that's fine. You've responded. Sorry, I won't interrupt any more.

HARRY: It's all too fatuous. I'm a member of the Goston Lawn Tennis Club. There.

MARY: Do you hold any office?

HARRY: No!

MARY: The Club is entirely devoted to tennis?

HARRY [*mumbles*]: We have social activities in winter.

MARY: Sorry?

HARRY: *We have social activities in winter.*

MARY: National Union of Journalists?

HARRY: Yes. I have to be.

MARY: Union office?

HARRY: I'm not militant.

MARY: Any other organisations?

HARRY: No.

MARY: Political?

HARRY: No.

MARY: Freemason?

HARRY: No.

MARY: No you won't say, or no-no.

HARRY: Just no.

MARY: Hobbies or non-professional skills?

HARRY: Minding my own business.

MARY: You keep yourself to yourself?

HARRY: I was being sarcastic.

MARY: You *don't* keep yourself to yourself?

HARRY: I do.

MARY: Non-political.

HARRY: I said so! I said I was not militant.

MARY: Ratepayers, Parent-teachers or any other?

HARRY [*struggling to keep cool*]: Yes, no and no, in that order. Just shut up a minute while I re-cap; large building with clinical features, to which I'm summoned to give a factual account of myself . . . [*Feverishly goes over the lack of evidence*]

MARY: So you say.

HARRY: So I say? Dammit, are you or are you not asking questions?

MARY: I am.

HARRY: About me?

MARY: Yes. Now, financial status?

HARRY: I will give information of that sort to the Inland Revenue and to no-one else.

MARY: And to a building society.

HARRY: All right, and to a building society.

MARY: To a bank manager? For a bank loan?

HARRY [*short*]: Yes. You always have to win of course.

MARY: It isn't a battle. I'm not insisting on information.

HARRY: Well this is your come-uppance anyway.

MARY: Simply asking questions.

HARRY: Damn personal ones.

MARY: Every set of circumstances has its rules, I was following them.

HARRY: Oh yes? But I didn't know the circumstances, nor am I likely to find out, am I? So far as I can see they're impossible and non-existent. I don't believe you had anything in mind, so let's scrub round it.

MARY: What about a set of circumstances where there are no circumstances?

HARRY: . . . is that a clue?

MARY: Could be.

HARRY: Oh for God's sake!

MARY: This place has rules. No smoking. Please turn off the lights when leaving the dressing room.

HARRY: Not too oppressive.

MARY: You observed them.

HARRY: I'm a law-abiding citizen.

MARY: Are there some rules you can't keep?

HARRY: I never keep New Year Resolutions, on principle.

MARY: What principle?

HARRY: The principle that I don't keep New Year Resolutions. There has to be limits, we're pushed around enough by others, no sense compounding the offence by doing it to yourself.

MARY: Rules are an offence, and self-discipline is the unforgivable offence.

HARRY [*cocky*]: Yes. Are we still where we are?

MARY: Oh yes. Suppose we change the rules?

HARRY: What rules? and who's we? Gettin' crafty, see?

MARY: We, all of us, everybody; and the rules are the things you can't do or must do.

HARRY: If we change 'em, I'll obey 'em. I'm one of we.

MARY: Most people believe in the Rule of Law. Most people say yes straight off to any rule and expect to be punished if they step over the line. If they avoid declaring their income, they would expect to be punished if they were caught.

HARRY: . . . if it was against the rules.

MARY: It is against the rules.

HARRY: I still won't declare it.

MARY: You defy the rules?

HARRY: All right, yes. Now punish me.

MARY: I don't punish. I record. Facts.

HARRY: *Punish* me, let's see your power.

MARY: I have no power.

HARRY: So how am I to be punished? [*His blood is racing, and his lips tremble, wet with excitement; like a racing swimmer at the end of his energy glancing at the runners-up he glances at the clock, chunking steadily on. Just masters himself*] Without the power to punish, who can punish me?

MARY: I have no power. [*Thoughtful*] I suppose I *could* create power for others.

HARRY [*pouncing*]: Facts are power, yes. Detailed comprehensive facts create power: so for whom do you record these facts? Some authority?

MARY: They are not for use, or for any particular person.

HARRY: There's some loophole here, and you're covering up.

ALISDAIR: I think you may be asking questions that Mary *can't* answer, Harry; am I with you, Mary?

HARRY: The government? The police?

ALISDAIR: Harry, please . . .

HARRY: Shut up.

ALISDAIR [*'manners'*]: Sorry.

MARY: The police could only use information if some crime had been committed.

HARRY: What? [*Shakily relieved, though not sure why*] Come off it, you haven't they haven't I haven't done anything. That's ludicrous. Alisdair, she's cheating. How can I possibly be required to give personal details to the police when I've done nothing? In no way transgressed?

ALISDAIR [*cool*]: I don't think Mary has said the police are concerned.

MARY: Have I asked you for a piece of information that no-one else has ever demanded?

HARRY *drags his chair abruptly back up to the table, picks up the blank sheet of scribbling paper from in front of* MARY, *and tears it up.*

HARRY: Give me that. Right.

HARRY *tosses the bits away.*

MARY: What did you do?

HARRY: What d'you mean? I tore up your notes.

MARY: That's my business to do that.

HARRY: Well I did it for you. [*Panting with excitement*] Good game, isn't it? I protested. I registered effective objection. I withheld certain information, defied punishment, and used violence to destroy evidence. Very interesting: not everybody can find out their point of protest. Thank you.

MARY: While you have been sitting here . . . ?

HARRY [*after waiting*]: Mm?

MARY: During the time you have been sitting here, what would you say has been happening to the children?

HARRY: I'd forgotten about them. With that attendant around the place. Have to have a word with the management about him.

MARY: The attendant came by?

HARRY: Yes. The attendant, the one I didn't like.

MARY: Could you describe him?

HARRY: All right. Hollow-eyed, drooping . . . yet sinewy, certainly sinewy; dark-complexioned, grizzled though not old. With a stooping steady walk. Not taking any notice of anything outside his duties.

MARY: Very good. Yes, I can see him.

HARRY: It was hard to tell whether he knew . . . or cared . . . that we were following. [HARRY's *rather pleased with his descriptive powers, and calmer*] What about him?

MARY: The attendant came?

HARRY: Yes? Come on? I hope he didn't frighten the children?

MARY: No.

HARRY: He couldn't touch them. No question of that.

MARY: Why couldn't he?

HARRY: He . . . what? Go on, he took them away? You can't disappear children. What did my wife do? Whistle a happy tune?

MARY: She wouldn't want to alarm the children.

HARRY [*not really attending*]: . . . sooner or later, we protest, whoever we are. Sorry, go on. No, don't go on, what is this? You can't rush around . . . can't whisk children along empty corridors, quiet. They're noisy objects, and anyway we've already said the attendant's old, slow-moving. They wouldn't get round the first corner. And, and the game breaks down b-because my wife would come after me when she missed them.

MARY: Are you sure? Having drawn a blank down the corridor, might she not hesitate in case you too had disappeared? As you hesitate to look?

HARRY [*stiff*]: It's possible.

MARY: Can we get on now?

HARRY: There's something very nasty about your mind, and I'm not tolerating it. What's the idea? Is this some kind of a world gone mad? Where did he take them?

MARY: Who?

HARRY: The children. The attendant. I suppose the proposition is he took them towards those ghastly . . . those thingies.

MARY: Surgical booths? We don't know where he took them.

HARRY: Oh yes? And why don't I go and look? Because there's nobody there. Nobody.

MARY: There'd be no point, would there? Can we get on?

HARRY: What do I do to get out?

MARY: Nothing.

HARRY: Right, I'm off. I give up.

MARY: No, you do nothing.

HARRY [*head beginning to spin*]: Ah. Yes, I see, well I won't, all right? Please, I don't feel too well. Can we go and have a cup of tea? And start another round? I had quite a good idea of some circumstances . . . [*Mumbles vaguely round the next few words before getting them right*] cir . . . circumstances . . . quite . . . Quite funny this one could be. Be an opportunity for you, Mary. We can stop the recording, can't we, Alisdair? Sorry.

MARY: You refuse to give your income, do you?

HARRY: Oh now please Mary, I've told you. It's not that I object, but that was the game. You said it was immaterial. I had no intentions of spoiling anything . . . it's not at all easy for me *to* stop, you can imagine, all the people w-watching . . . but give up now darling, I've had it. Head's going boing boing boing.

ALISDAIR: Could he have a glass of water, Mary?

MARY: Of course.

ALISDAIR *gets it for him . . . genial . . . all good human stuff this.*

HARRY: Thanks, that's just what I do need. [*Drinks*] Well, Mary, you had me there. You certainly have got a nasty mind.

MARY: How?

HARRY [*dizzily*]: Oh all that about the attendant, the kids, surgery. Frightful.

MARY: You invented it.

HARRY [*somehow he can't get enough oxygen*]: Well, we can listen to a playback and find that out, can't we?

MARY: Can we reel back, Alisdair?

ALISDAIR: What's that?

MARY: Can we listen to what's already recorded now?

ALISDAIR: Oh. I suppose I could ask. [*Goes*] I'll see.

HARRY: Anyway I don't see that it matters whose head it was brewed in; it was in pretty evil taste.

MARY: Now, what is your annual income?

HARRY [*distressed, cornered*]: I'm now on two thousand five hundred, all right? You'll have to work out my fees from this for yourself. Just please leave it alone.

MARY: It worries you to have to tell how much you earn?

HARRY: It's not that, of course it isn't, I tell you I'm not feeling too good. The recording's messed up, so please leave it alone.

[*Suddenly* HARRY *is galvanized by a nasty thought*] Surely to God they've stopped the recording! Alisdair!

MARY: Investments? [*Pause*] Investments? Are you still there?

HARRY: Eh? Of course I'm still here. What is this?

ALISDAIR [*returning*]: Mary, excuse me, we can reel back up to the last reel, the one we're on now. Anything particular you want?

MARY [*pitching up*]: Anything that's handy, recording room! Can you hear me?

ENGINEER [*on P.A., loud and clear, with a pause and a click each time as he switches over the talk-back*]: Right.

MARY: Then I can tell you whether to reel on or back for the bit we want!

ALISDAIR: They were most co-operative. Really rather excited I think.

Over the P.A. we hear the mike roar and bump as HARRY *dragged his chair abruptly back up to the table, and the scribbling pad was grabbed and the top sheet torn and scattered; then* HARRY'*s voice:*

[HARRY: Give me that. Right.

MARY: What did you do?

HARRY: What d'you mean? I tore up your notes.

MARY: That's my business to do that.

HARRY: Well I did it for you. [*Panting with excitement*] Good game, isn't it? I protested. I registered effective objection. I withheld certain information, defied punishment, and used violence to destroy evidence. . . .]

MARY [*meanwhile, tries to interrupt this last speech, but can't until the* ENGINEER *is listening with the playback off*]: Reel on a bit, recording room! Recording room!

ENGINEER [*over the P.A.*]: Sorry. [*Clicks off*]

MARY: Reel on a bit from there and try again.

Chittering over the P.A. as the tape is run on, then:

[MARY: Could you describe him?

HARRY: All right. Hollow-eyed, drooping . . . yet sinewy, certainly sinewy; dark-complexioned, grizzled though not old. With a stooping steady walk. Not taking any notice of anything outside his duties.

MARY: Very good. Yes. I can see him.

HARRY: It was hard to tell whether he knew . . . or cared . . .

that we were following. [HARRY's *rather pleased with his descriptive powers, and calmer*] What about him?

MARY: The attendant came?]

HARRY [*tries to interrupt, but the tape spins on*]: All right. All right, I said! Point taken!

He shakes his head free from the embarrassment of shouting up, when it was MARY *he was addressing. Meanwhile the tape plays on over the P.A.:*

[HARRY: Yes? Come on. I hope he didn't frighten the children?

MARY: No.

HARRY: He couldn't touch them. No question of that.

MARY: Why couldn't he?

HARRY: He . . . what? Go on, he took them away? You can't disappear children.]

ENGINEER: That all right? [*Click off to listen*]

MARY: Thank you, recording room! [*Turns to* HARRY] Now, what was the other thing you didn't invent?

HARRY: Skip it.

MARY: Surgery, yes. [*Speaks up*] Recording room! Could we try right at the top of the show? Just a little way in? I think that's where I want!

HARRY: Yes. All right, fine. Now then, I take your point that I contributed my own . . .

MARY: Persecution?

HARRY [*struggling*]: No, no, not persecution ... because nothing actually happened to me . . . [*He wishes he could get that friendly grin off his face*] ... em ... threats.

MARY: Terror?

Pause. HARRY *glances up at the clock, chunking on. The P.A. fades up with:*

[HARRY: . . . rather like a hospital, isn't it?]

. . . *and out again.*

MARY: On a bit from that!

We hear the chittering of the tape over the P.A. as:

MARY: Terror, were you thinking?

Over the P.A. we hear:

[MARY: You saw surgical booths?

HARRY: Did I? Oh yes. Yes, so I did. Must have done, walking by, following the attendant . . . *etc.*]

HARRY [*pounces as soon as he hears* MARY's *recorded voice suggesting the booths*]: There! You said that! That was your filthy suggestion!

MARY: Reel back from there! Just a little!

HARRY: Don't dodge, that *was* your notion, a naked threat.

ENGINEER [*over the P.A.*]: Back from there? [*Click over*]

MARY: A few seconds back!

HARRY [*muttering, sweating*]: Irresponsible, completely messing it all up, the game.